FILMMAKERS SERIES

edited by
ANTHONY SLIDE

With my compliments
Harry Langdon

HARRY LANGDON

by
WILLIAM SCHELLY

FILMMAKERS, No. 3

The Scarecrow Press, Inc.
Metuchen, N.J., & London
1982

Frontispiece: portrait of Langdon <u>circa</u> THE CHASER (1928)
(from the Michael Copner Collection)

Hml
PN
1998
A3
L364967
1982

Library of Congress Cataloging in Publication Data

Schelly, William, 1951-
    Harry Langdon.

    (Filmmakers ; no. 3)
    Filmography: p.
    Bibliography: p.
    Includes index.
    1. Langdon, Harry, 1884-1944. I. Title.
II. Series: Filmmakers (Scarecrow Press) ;
no. 3.
PN1998.A3L364967 1982   791.43'028'0924 [B]
ISBN 0-8108-1567-2   82-6035

CONTENTS

ACKNOWLEDGMENTS

My sincerest appreciation and thanks to the following people and institutions:

> The Museum of Modern Art (Charles Silver, Mary Corliss)
> The American Film Institute (Lawrence Karr)
> The Los Angeles Public Library (Tom Owen)
> The Library of Congress Copyright Office (John T. Wayne)
> The Seattle Public Library (Ruth Webb)
> The King County Public Library
> The University of Washington (several libraries)

For their valuable assistance and encouragement: Walter Kerr, Fred Lawrence Guiles, Bessie Love, Joe Rock, Fifi D'Orsay, Diana Cary, Michael Barrier, Murray Glass, Mavis Goetsch, Richard Minot, Chuck Jones, Bruce Gardiner, Colleen Moore, and Wayne Powers.

I am particularly indebted to Marcel Marceau for his participation in this project.

Day-to-day moral support came from Edward Brooks, Terry Martell, Allen DeShong, and Diana Borasio. Their suggestions shaped the manuscript more than they know.

I would also like to thank Mabel Langdon. Although she did not contribute to my book, our several conversations gave me a sense of contact with Harry. Her efforts to collect and preserve films, stills and other Langdon memorabilia are highly laudable.

My special thanks go to the following people:

Anthony Slide, for providing an encouraging professional assessment and helping extensively with the filmography.

James Holt, for allowing me access not only to his great library of film books but to his phenomenal expertise on the Silent Era. I am deeply indebted to Stephanie Ogle (owner of Cinema Books in Seattle) for introducing me to Jim.

Michael Copner, for generously contributing all his information and several stills to this volume, even though he had been planning his own Langdon book. It helped immensely to have another Langdon maniac around. Many of Mike's highly original insights found their way into the manuscript. Mr. Cranston, take a bow.

William Schelly
Seattle, 1982

EDITOR'S NOTE

Along with Chaplin, Keaton, and Lloyd, Harry Langdon has long been considered one of the mainstays of silent screen comedy. It is surprising, therefore, that until now the comedian has not been the subject of a book-length study. His silent features, such as Tramp, Tramp, Tramp, The Strong Man, and Long Pants, illustrate Langdon's unique comedic qualities, and despite the efforts of his critics to denigrate his sound features, Langdon is surprisingly entertaining in A Soldier's Plaything and Hallelujah, I'm a Bum, among others. Perhaps the problem has been that Langdon's silent career has been closely interlinked with that of director Frank Capra, and it has become fashionable to praise the latter to the detriment of the former.

This book is not only the first on Langdon, but also a first for its thirty-year-old, Seattle-based author, William Schelly. Schelly has carefully studied all of Langdon's films --features and shorts, silent and sound--and provides a fresh insight into the qualities that made Langdon such an enduring star. James Agee's much quoted comment was that "Langdon had one queerly toned, unique little reed. But out of it he could get incredible melodies." Those "incredible melodies" may be heard once more in this seminal study of the life and work of Harry Langdon.

Anthony Slide

Chapter One: THE LATE BLOOMER

By 1923, Vaudeville was dying. The variety format--a compendium of jugglers, vocalists, animal acts, and comics-- was the most popular form of mass entertainment in the United States at the turn of the century. The two-a-day was cut down in its prime by a series of silvery shadows projected on a screen.

Economics made the movies more attractive for everyone concerned. Tickets were cheaper, overhead was lower, salaries were higher, and audiences were broader. Almost solely visual at first (with few dialogue titles), films naturally appealed to the burgeoning immigrant populations of the country. As early as 1910, film theaters outnumbered vaudeville outlets.

Nevertheless, the big city variety palaces, the glittering shrines that showcased the best of the vaudeville performers, still attracted large audiences that were not ready to give up the excitement and immediacy of live entertainment. Large population centers all had such venues. In Los Angeles, the most important was the Orpheum.

The Orpheum Theater, located at South Broadway and 6th Street (still standing, although it was re-named The Palace in 1926 when the new Orpheum Theater opened), was built by the Orpheum Theater and Realty Company and opened in June 1911. Like most of the twentieth-century houses on the circuit, it was in what is now known as "Beaux Arts" style, but was considered classical architecture and design in 1911. It originally seated 1,489 patrons.

1

The Orpheum stood near the heart of the growing film colony. The best seats went to the new royalty of the cinema, the kings and queens of the magical silent screen: Fairbanks, Pickford, Gish, Swanson, Chaplin. Also in regular attendance were the movie moguls, the names behind the names: Zukor, Laemmle, Sennett, Fox, Griffith. Applause from such a stellar audience was a heady elixir indeed.

It was decidedly unusual when comedian Harry Langdon, a twenty-year veteran of the vaudeville stage, felt less than the usual excitement when he arrived in Los Angeles in March of 1923 to headline a week at the Orpheum. Langdon was considering quitting show business, a decision he could not have made lightly.

Could he really give up the business of entertaining people, when that was all he had ever known? Show business had provided him with a way out of an austere childhood, given him a profession, kept money in his pockets, and put him in front of an endless parade of audiences. He had never aspired to anything else.

*   *   *

Harry Langdon was born on June 15, 1884, in Council Bluffs, Iowa, the son of Salvation Army workers. He grew up across the Missouri River in Omaha, where his parents were able to eke out only the barest of livings. Langdon himself repeated stories of his early near-poverty, and Salvation Army records indicate that his parents were simply humble workers in the Army. By the time Harry was ten years old, he found himself hawking the Omaha Bee on the street corners of the teaming midwestern metropolis.

Omaha in the 1880's was booming. With increasing commerce on the Missouri, and with the railroad through the Platte Valley having been completed just a decade earlier, the population grew tenfold between 1870 and 1890. Although Omaha could in no sense be considered cosmopolitan, Langdon was a city boy.

One of young Langdon's street corners where he sold papers was located in the theatrical district of town, a mishmash of burlesque joints, "legit" theaters, and penny arcades. Always on the lookout for extra money, the enterprising youth began doing odd jobs for the theater owners. The shy, near-sighted boy (who wore specs) was irresistibly drawn to the glamour of live theater and wanted to be part of it. He found acceptance among the worldly show business folk who befriended him.

Langdon didn't often get friendship from his peers. He spent all his spare money on theatrical make-up, phoney moustaches and nose putty, hoping to impress them. The ploy backfired. His play-acting only set him apart from the less imaginative kids.

He even played truant from Sunday school (surely a risky matter, given his parents' strict religious beliefs) to help the bill-posters plaster barns and fences with colorful announcements of the latest coming attractions.

One of Harry's first jobs inside a theater was prop boy at a local Opry House. He had a lot to learn. He infuriated the manager when the centurions of Caeser (in a cornfed version of Quo Vadis) marched on stage carrying Revolutionary muskets. Fortunately, he was agile enough to avoid trouble by climbing into the rigging above the stage, safely out of reach.

Langdon would take any job to be near the theatrical world. He sold tickets, worked as a concessionaire and even assisted a theater janitor. "My parents couldn't afford to give me money for theater tickets but I always managed in some way to see most of the shows," he later recalled. "When I was twelve years old I got my job as an usher. The only pay I got was the privilege of watching the show when I wasn't seating customers, but I was satisfied. "[1] Langdon was an usher at the Doheney Theater in Council Bluffs.

Soon Harry yearned to perform more than anything else. All the time he was working backstage, he would make anyone available laugh with routines both borrowed and original. When a local outlet inaugurated a series of amateur nights, Harry was ready. His planned ineptitude reportedly brought the house down that evening in 1896. He continued appearing on amateur nights sporadically for nearly a year.

Then Langdon had his first "solid" job offer. Shortly after celebrating his thirteenth birthday, Harry asked his parents if he could leave home to take a job with Dr. Belcher's Kickapoo Indian Medicine Show. Surprisingly, his mother accepted his decision. She even packed his trunk and gave him her blessing.

In a way, Harry Langdon lived the fantasy of many boys: leaving home to join the circus, for the traveling medicine show most resembled a scaled-down circus. An august personage purporting to be a man of medicine would welcome the townspeople to a hastily assembled big top and extoll the amazing healing properties of his own unique brand of therapeutic elixir. When the commercial portion of the evening was completed, and the evening's proceeds were safely locked in a safe in the Doc's railroad car, the show would commence.

It turned out that Langdon exhibited an amazing proficiency in nearly every aspect of the show. During his early teenage years with several medicine shows, he tried his hand at everything. For a time he was a featured juggler. He played banjo and other instruments in the band. (Supposedly, Langdon had the ability to play any musical instrument by ear.) Sometimes he would rub burnt cork on his face and do a minstrel turn. He played comical Germans, Jews, and Irishmen. The young performer managed to pick up some simple soft-shoe and tap routines, and sang in a high, reedy voice. These early modest efforts met with gratifying acceptance. Harry Langdon made the grade.

When the show wound down for the night, the troupe would pull up stakes, pack up the "top" and move on to the next population center. If few were healed by the much-touted tonic, most people at least got their money's worth of songs, dances and novelty acts. The shows were unfailingly popular, especially because they concentrated on the smaller towns where entertainment of any kind was welcome.

But Harry didn't leave home for good. His first foray lasted a mere six months. When he didn't get paid, Langdon returned to Omaha where he began performing at Mickey Mullin's Music Hall. For the next few years, he continued returning home between jobs.

Langdon developed into an artist of real ability. A talented doodler from his earliest years, he possessed an uncanny knack for caricature. He created a little comic character which he later described as the first prototype for his simple-minded screen persona: baggy trousers, a too-small hat, a round face, and big innocent eyes. Recognizing his ability, his parents encouraged him to make his living as a cartoonist.

Langdon portrait (taken after he became famous) harkens back to his early career days as a circus clown.   (Academy Collection)

During one respite from the road, the editor of a local newspaper invited him to submit his artwork. Langdon landed a job as a staff cartoonist and illustrator. He enjoyed all forms of the American joke, and was intrigued by the differing qualities of the newspaper strip. He later told Photoplay,[2]

> Newspaper comics are hard because you have four or five frames in which to tell your comedy. You don't have the elbow room of the circus, the stage or the screen.
> On the other hand, you can get away with jokes in your strip that would be censored as too violent and brutal on the screen. Somehow the public doesn't think it's brutal when they see a ton of coal fall on a fat policeman in a newspaper comic, but they would send you to jail ... if you tried it on the screen.

When Langdon became famous, William Randolph Hearst offered him $3,000 a week to draw a daily strip for his newspaper syndicate. Although the offer was a blatant attempt to exploit Harry's popularity as a movie clown, he certainly had the experience to complete the assignment with professionalism and assurance.

But Langdon never forgot the theater. He kept his hand in by acting in local melodramas like East Lynne. It was never long before the wanderlust would hit him, a job would be offered, and he'd be packing his trunk again.

For a few seasons he worked as a circus clown and tumbler for the Hamburg and Wallace circus, and later did a stint as a trapeze artist. He was an expert ventriloquist. Backstage he was a barber, a sign painter, and an excellent carpenter. In short, he was a very handy, resourceful young man to have around any type of traveling show.

In 1899, at fifteen, Langdon teamed up with another young man and went on the road in vaudeville. Actually, he tried most of the formats then available: burlesque, musical comedy, minstrel shows. He performed a chair-balancing specialty during his period with the well-known Gus Sun Minstrels.

The year 1903 was an important one for Harry. At the age of nineteen, he met and eloped with Rose Frances

Mensolf. They formed a team (she had been a musical comedy actress when they met) and Langdon wrote the comedy
act that became their bread and butter for the next twenty
years: "Johnny's New Car. "

This well-known act began with Harry and Rose "driving" onstage in a wooden breakaway car, with the nickname
"Baby" on the license plate. The balky flivver would then
stall in front of a hospital set (a cloth drop). Rose played
the shrewish wife to Harry's meek, helpless little husband.

As the engine "exploded" and steam shot skyward,
Harry's every effort would systematically worsen his predicament. Just when he thought he had the radiator fixed, the
car wouldn't start. Then the fenders would fall off, the door
would come off in his hands and his wife's temper would ex-
plode again. With the automobile a newfangled, slightly ridiculous phenomenon, audiences loved it.

The Langdons performed "Johnny's New Car" thousands
of times, with mounting success, on the Orpheum and Keith
vaudeville circuits. How could they have stuck with the same
act for twenty years? On television, a performer must constantly introduce new material; in vaudeville, an actor could
perform for three years and never in the same town twice.
Audiences actually welcomed familiar acts, for they were a
proven quantity on the bill. [3]

The virtue of that kind of repetition was that an act,
usually no longer than fifteen minutes in length, could be
honed to perfection. The comedians knew exactly where the
laughs would come. Their material was lovingly nurtured,
with every nuance planned to give the appearance of sponta-
neity. Langdon recalled,

> One valuable little thing I learned in vaudeville is
> that you can pretty well control the laughter of
> your crowd. If things were going well, I'd play
> along at a fairly slow tempo and keep my voice
> well down. If the laughs were too few and quiet,
> I'd increase my speed and raise my voice. It
> seemed to be infectious, for almost always it would
> make them laugh louder and longer. [4]

Although the Langdons made a fair living at vaudeville,
they discovered over the years that it was extremely difficult
to get ahead. What money they made was quickly eaten up

by travel expenses.   And they had to face the fact that their
act had reached a plateau in popularity.   They weren't going
to get any bigger.

In fact, the vaudeville decline made jobs more difficult than ever to secure, as theaters closed or changed over
to movie palaces.   Steady work, once taken for granted, was
far from certain.   Putting together a continuous circuit
through the smaller towns had become particularly difficult,
and it was not always possible to work exclusively in the
bigger cities where variety remained relatively healthy.

Besides, Harry and Rose were pushing forty.   They
were tired of their nomadic lifestyle and felt it was time to
get away from cheap food, jerkwater trains, and a different
bed every week.   The urge to settle down became stronger.
There was talk of starting a sign-painting business, or a return to cartooning and illustration.   Harry Langdon was never
a man without possibilities.

As for a career in films, Harry surely must have
recognized that a producer or talent scout might catch the
act and offer him a contract.   But Langdon had played Los
Angeles dozens of times before.   There had been no mad
rush to sign him up.   While Harry considered his various
options and prepared to take the Orpheum stage one evening
in March 1923, he could not have known that his luck was
about to change.

*   *   *

Mack Sennett is widely given credit for discovering Harry
Langdon for films.   This is not (strictly speaking) the truth.
Unexpectedly, comedian Harold Lloyd was Harry's early champion.   Lloyd's screen characterization of a bespectacled go-
getter was near its peak in popularity.   In his World of
Comedy, Lloyd recalled: "I originally saw [Langdon] doing
an act called Johnny's New Car, and I told [comedy film pro-
ducer] Hal Roach that he would make a good comic for films.
Hal went down to the Orpheum ... and saw Harry, and he
agreed. " Roach, the only competitor that Sennett acknowledged, was in the process of building his own film empire
which would (in the next five years) overtake Sennett's own
studio.   In his OUR GANG series, Roach generated laughter
with more personality-oriented material than Sennett used;
his style might have perfectly suited Harry's talents.

Hal Roach offered Langdon a contract. Harry was receptive, but negotiations broke down. Langdon wanted $100 more a week than the producer felt he was worth. However, Harry's luck was running high. A second offer came on the heels of the first. Apparently, the salary was higher ($250 a week escalating to $1000 a week for ten short comedies, plus 10 percent of the profits) and Langdon immediately accepted.

The man who signed Harry Langdon was named Sol Lesser. Lesser was a young independent producer who distributed D. W. Griffith's HEARTS OF THE WORLD (1918) and signed Jackie Coogan. He starred "The Kid" in six pictures, including OLIVER TWIST (1922).

On March 29, the contract was signed. Harry would have his film career. When Lesser's Principal Pictures Corporation officially announced the signing, Lloyd again lent his praise: "Langdon has the makings of an excellent screen comedian. He's bound to succeed and I wish him all the luck in the world. I will look forward and follow his progress before the camera with great interest. " The two comedians became friends.

The United Lot, probably the largest and best equipped leasing studio in Burbank, was selected as the production site for the new comedy series. Alf Goulding, earlier a comedian and director of Lloyd's Roach comedies, was hired to direct THE SKYSCRAPER, an airplane story written by Langdon. The series was moving into production when Lesser made a surprise move. He sold Harry's contract to Mack Sennett.

"Johnny's New Car" was committed to film around this time, most likely by Lesser. Sennett was impressed. He saw something, an undefinable quality, that made Harry Langdon special. On the strength of his performance in this film, Sennett agreed to pay an undisclosed sum to Lesser for Langdon's services. By December 1923 Langdon found himself obliged to report for work in Edendale at the Mack Sennett Studios.

By the time Harry passed through the gate of Sennett's lot, the parameters of the producer's slapstick style had been established. The early Keystone comedies provided the formula, causing howls of laughter with a pie in the face, a

kick in the pants, or a clunk on the head. When this pattern
of comical violence became popular, Sennett repeated similar
gags endlessly during the decade that followed. By 1923 they
had become predictable.

Sennett's comic vision was limited. Instead of opting
for subtlety and nuance, the only real way to make a finite
number of gag situations seem fresh and original, he simply
added more and bigger versions of the same visual jokes.
Instead of a clunk on the head, for example, he substituted
a sudden jolt of electricity--in essence, the same thing.

It wasn't only the Sennett films that had reached a
creative cul-de-sac by the early 1920's. Vitagraph's Larry
Semon is almost an object lesson in how a comic's over-
reliance on formula (Sennett-derived) could destroy a career.
A former cartoonist and director, Semon achieved considerable popularity in the 1918-1922 period with his little, white-
faced alter ego.

Semon stated frequently that a comedian was only as
good as his gags. Rumor had it that the famous black note-
book he kept in his hip pocket contained a million dollars
worth of funny ideas. But as audiences grew familiar with
his version of screen farce, Semon was obliged to spend
more and more money to make gags bigger and (theoretically)
funnier. He eventually spent so heavily that his films couldn't
hope to make a profit.

No new major comedians emerged in the early 1920's.
Dozens took their shot at it, either in Edendale or at such
rival studios as Roach, Fox, and Christie. Most worked
variations on the original Keystone formula and were rarely
able to break out of the huge field.

Sennett himself had lost his original stars. At various
times, he produced films starring Fatty Arbuckle, Mabel Normand, Charlie Chaplin, Marie Dressler, Wallace Beery, Raymond Griffith, and Slim Summerville. Most of them, propelled by their initial success with Sennett, found greater ac-
claim, heightened artistic achievement, and bigger salaries
in their subsequent endeavors. Sennett was tight with a buck,
and it had proved to be his undoing.

When his stars walked out, Sennett howled: "QUIT!
All of you! I can get up my own stories, build my own sets,
photograph and direct my own pictures, and act the lead in
them too. QUIT AND BE DAMNED!!"[5]

He brought in new stars: Ben Turpin, Billy Bevan, Chester Conklin, Bull Montana, and Andy Clyde. None of them showed anything of the great talent of his early discoveries.

Only three major comedians maintained their level of creativity and popularity into the 1920's, and Sennett didn't have any of them: Buster Keaton, Harold Lloyd, and Charlie Chaplin.

Keaton, a vaudevillian from the time he could walk, rose to prominence in Fatty Arbuckle's Comique series in 1917. His innovative, craftsmanlike films earned him a loyal following, but his popularity leveled off with OUR HOSPITALITY (1924). The Great Stone Face had become perhaps too familiar; the critics began carping that Buster was repeating himself, although in truth each new film was different in tone and style from the last.

Lloyd's career very nearly paralleled that of his famous screen character. Energy and ambition propelled him to the front ranks. He supervised the best gag men in the business and could have shared Sennett's dilemma except that he recognized the importance of integrating character and action. Still, his comedies were basically an elaboration of the Keystone formula. As an actor, Lloyd was a great technician, but he lacked imagination and depth.

Chaplin had troubles of his own. The Little Tramp had been accepted as a cultural icon by virtually the entire world. Intensely aware of his exalted status in the industry, he became self-conscious and his output turned to a trickle. In 1923 he directed a film (A WOMAN OF PARIS) in which he made only a cameo appearance, out of his Tramp costume. He did not return to the screen until THE GOLD RUSH, two years later.

Sennett knew that there was room at the top and wanted nothing more than a new feather in his cap. He dreamed of finding a special new comedian who could equal Chaplin, though he was not looking for a Tramp imitator like Billy West. The next big star would have to be different. The public was ready for something new. Then Sennett found Langdon.

NOTES

1.   Los Angeles Record, December 10, 1930.

2. *Photoplay*, June 1925.
3. The Langdons performed other material sporadically, in-
    cluding a routine called "After the Ball."
4. *Photoplay*, June 1925, p. 126.
5. Fowler, Gene. *Father Goose*. New York: Covici Friede
    Publishers, 1934, p. 287.

Chapter Two: HIS FALSE START

Landing a contract with Mack Sennett was a step up for Harry Langdon. Despite having sown the seeds of future failure, Sennett was still producing highly successful comedies. Harry's contract with Principal Pictures provided a humble entrance into the film industry; his reassignment to Edendale substantially increased his chances of making an impact. Now Langdon had the ample resources of Sennett's comedy kingdom in his corner.

He would receive far more media exposure at a major studio. The well-oiled publicity machine would, at Sennett's signal, bombard the media with a storm of press releases and photographs. Sennett himself was a famous personality and master promoter whose dictums instantly produced headlines in trade journals and newspapers around the country. Shortly after acquiring Langdon's services, the Los Angeles Morning Telegraph (Dec. 20, 1923) wasted no time in announcing: "Mack Sennett says he has a new comedy find [who] has the potentialities of a Chaplin. "

Finances were never a problem. Although nominally accountable to his two partners (Charles Bauman and Adam Kessel), Sennett could spend money as he saw fit. At the same time, costs could be minimized by using many standing sets and employing assembly-line production methods.

Sennett's excellent distribution deal with the worldwide Pathe film exchange guaranteed that Harry's films would reach hundreds of thousands of people in virtually every film market. No independent distributor, even Sol Lesser, could hope

to do better.   Simply being under the Sennett banner assured
that a film would make a profit, provided production costs
could be kept under control.   The flashing of the famous
name on theater screens still evoked applause and a receptive, happy audience.   When Lesser sold the contract to Sennett, Harry may have been temporarily disoriented, but he
could hardly have failed to appreciate the obvious advantages
provided by his new boss.

By the time Harry Langdon came to films, the standard comedy format was the two-reeler, about twenty minutes
in length.   Even though dramatic films had long since expanded to a seventy-minute average, the shorter running time
remained the most popular for comedy.   Literally thousands
of two-reelers were produced between 1912 and 1955.

Just because they were briefer than features didn't
mean short comedies were looked down upon.   Two-reelers
provided the proving ground for all the great silent clowns,
even though a select few were graduating to longer formats.
Often the comedy featurette was the most popular item on
the bill.   Every theater program had to include a comedy.

One of Harry's first Sennett two-reelers was SMILE
PLEASE (1924), in which he played an energetic, fumbling
portrait photographer.   In his small-town studio, Harry engages in a battle of wits with a bratty kid (a Sennett stock
character).   Langdon, clad in a jaunty striped coat and straw
skimmer, desperately tries to tame the spoiled child, while
trying to snap a family portrait.   The ornery kid has other
ideas.

For starters, he bites Harry's finger.   Before long,
he plants a skunk inside the big box-shaped camera.   Harry
disappears under the shroud to snap the photo; seconds later,
he sinks senseless to the floor.   So does the camera, on
tripod legs that turn rubbery.

Harry gets his revenge.   He watches as the irate
mother-in-law attacks the boy's father.   Each time she
swings, he ducks and the blows hit the curtain behind him.
With neat dispatch, Harry holds the kid's backside up to the
back of the curtain, and the spoiled urchin receives what
may be his first spanking.

Strangely, Langdon also doubles for town Sheriff, as
if two separate stories had been pasted together.   Lawman

HIS NEW MAMA (Sennett/Pathe, 1924). (The Museum of Modern Art, New York City)

Harry engages in some nonsensical mock-heroics involving a suspected burglar. In a breathless rescue, Harry carries a bundled figure from his burning office building. He fondles the huddled figure. But when the blanket pulls aside, it is his moustached rival. Harry quickly covers the man again, returns him to the burning building and rescues the girl instead.

SMILE PLEASE is not without amusing moments, but very few originate with Langdon. No one was quite sure how Langdon would project on the screen or what sort of character he would best portray. He looks uncomfortable, even unpleasant, in a wedding sequence where his shirt front keeps flipping up into his face. He walks with a stiff mechanical gait like a wind-up doll. His character starts on promising ground during the photo session, but unaccountably shifts when he becomes the Sheriff. His facial expressions lack subtlety, conveying simple surprise, anger, or exasperation.

Any reasonably competent comic could have played Harry's role to much the same effect. The comedian is simply one element of a dominant master plan. Director Roy Del Ruth focuses on the execution of the individual visual gags. Instead of building out of the human relationships, they exist in and of themselves.

Many of the gags depend on Sennett's penchant for visual trickery. A hat hops when the wearer is startled. Cars jump over fences. Bodies fly through the air in unlikely trajectories. These stunts, accomplished through off-screen manipulation, are called "wire gags." A wire gag, by its very components, looked artificial.

At one point in SMILE PLEASE, Harry sneezes. The entire rug flies into the air, covering his photo subjects. All impossibility. Sennett found these gimmicks hilarious, and maybe audiences did, too--for a time. Viewed from a current perspective, the novelty quickly palls. They beg too hard for the laugh. Their presence in Langdon's films belies Sennett's grandiose claim that he had a new comedian of Chaplinesque stature, for Charlie rarely had need for such desperate measures.

In Sennett's autobiography, "modestly" titled King of Comedy, he later admitted: "It was difficult for us at first to know how to use Langdon, accustomed as we were to firing the gags and the falls at the audience as fast as possible."

Sennett was capable of understanding that individual comedians needed material specifically tailored to their unique talent. It wasn't enough that cross-eyed Ben Turpin could throw a pie, perform a double-take or do a credible pratfall. Turpin didn't rise above mediocrity until they found the perfect character fix: burlesques of heroic figures and romantic leading men (and women). At first, finding a "handle" for Langdon proved elusive.

As a result, the early Langdon comedies adhere strictly to Sennett formula, where the gag reigned supreme. These films (SHANGHAIED LOVERS, FLICKERING YOUTH, THE CAT'S MEOW) are crammed with many variations of slapstick buffoonery with very little care or consistency. How funny can a film be when the viewer has no definite feeling of character from the star comedian?

Now Harry was learning the disadvantages of working for Sennett. A comedian had very little to say about the comedies that bore his name, less when he was new on the lot. Sennett liked to separate creative functions as much as possible.

The writing was confined mostly to the gag room on the top floor of Sennett's administration building, known as the Tower. Ideas never left the building if Sennett hadn't laughed when he first heard them. Directors rarely took part in initial story conferences; they were summoned to Sennett's sanctum only after he had approved his writers' concoctions. Writers were forbidden to visit the set.

And actors? Actors were to be seen and not heard, both on screen and off. Sennett suspiciously regarded them as prima donnas whose demands gave him constant headaches and who were too ambitious for their own good. The Old Man (Sennett's nickname) loved his comics, but stubbornly resisted the rising influence and importance of individual stars. Their input was generally discouraged. In his autobiography, Chaplin recalled Sennett's putdown: "Just do what you're told and we'll be satisfied." His philosophy hadn't altered noticeably since 1914.

If anyone had bothered to consult Langdon, he could have provided the basis of a possible screen character. After all, he had spent the past twenty years fighting a balky stage auto, perfecting a series of hesitant, insecure mannerisms. His child/man character had always gotten laughs from his reactions to comical conflict.

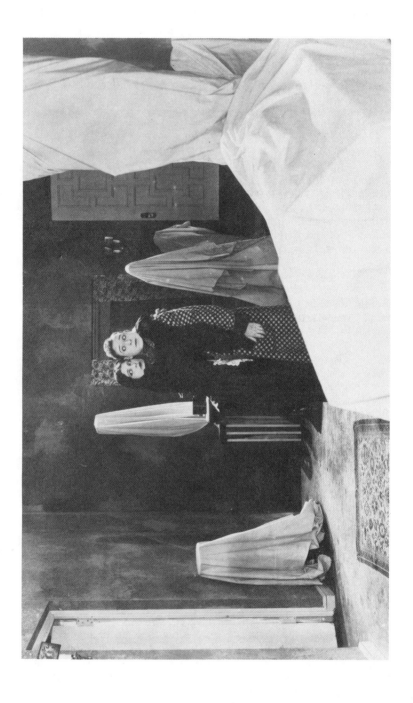

If Harry spoke up, he was undoubtedly assured that everything was being done to guarantee his success, and like Chaplin he should do what he was told. Harry had little choice but to acquiesce; his contract did not specify script approval. From time to time, he must have yearned to be back on the vaudeville stage where he was the sole architect of his performance.

PICKING PEACHES (1924) follows the same general form as SMILE PLEASE. This time Harry portrays a clumsy shoe clerk whose inept handling of a ladder leaves him hanging on the side of the building. Although married, Harry has a roving eye and ends up frolicking on the beach with some typical Sennett bathing girls. His wife's discovery of his philandering provides the impetus for most of the action that propels the film to its conclusion.

One sequence stands out. Harry is forced to hide under the covers in a strange bedroom, only to have the man of the house climb into bed with him. Harry's facial reactions --tremulous fear, eyes widening with shock--show personality. His dilemma in itself is funnier than the harsher physical abuse he suffered. For those few fleeting moments, his acting ability and Sennett's gag situation successfully work together.

Certainly this brief scene seems extraordinary only through the advantage of hindsight. The sexual role-reversal suggested in this bedroom mix-up takes on added significance because Harry explored that territory much further in later, more accomplished films.

Still, PICKING PEACHES engages the viewer better than SMILE, PLEASE. Marital comedy, even though predictable, put Langdon in the kind of human context in which he excelled. Although he later proved that he could succeed outside a domestic milieu, he constantly returned to that setting throughout his career.

Sennett's writers were unimpressed with Harry Langdon. His respectable vaudeville reputation hadn't reached them. They wondered aloud what the Old Man saw in an anemic-looking, middle-aged comic who had played tank towns

[Opposite:] THE FIRST HUNDRED YEARS (Sennett/Pathe, 1924). (The Museum of Modern Art, New York City)

for twenty years.   Had Sennett finally gone off the deep end?
Sure, he had discovered some big stars.   But ... Langdon?

Sennett was adamant.   Even though he had started as
a writer at Biograph, he lacked the ability to articulate what
he saw in Langdon.   Yet he did not hesitate to put his reputation on the line in advertising and promotional releases.
Sennett was a gambler.   After years of being proved right,
he believed his hunches.

Realizing he was in trouble, Langdon contacted Harold
Lloyd and explained the difficulties he was having on the Sennett lot.   He just wasn't scoring with the public.   Lloyd ad-
vised him to slow down the pace.   Sennett was working Harry
too fast, Harold observed.   He had done the same thing at
first with Chaplin.

Although Langdon agreed, his influence on the subsequent films was as limited as ever.   Even his acting was
manipulated by "experienced" directors.   The gags he was
given were mainly the product of comedy hack writers.   One
could easily get by at Sennett with only the slightest amount
of imagination, and many did.   The writers endlessly re-
cycled threadbare plots and rarely formulated scenarios with
real wit.   Many of the directors were no better.

Despite the many faults in Sennett's production system,
it would be an oversimplification to place all the blame on
his shoulders.   Harry Langdon, like all the enduring silent
fantasists, needed time to find his screen character.

Although the Little Tramp appeared as early as Chaplin's second film, he didn't hit his stride for two more years
(the Mutual period).   Buster Keaton broke his stone face with
a wide grin in early Comique comedies.   Lloyd also spent
several years obliquely imitating Chaplin with his Lonesome
Luke series until he hit upon his "glasses character. "

These comedians were lucky to get an early start.
They had time for hit and miss experimentation.   Until the
end of the First World War, audiences were less discrimi-
nating and quantity was more important than quality.   But in
the 1920's, silent film moved into its golden age.   Scripts,
photography and acting all rose to a higher level of profes-
sionalism and polish.   The public was choosier and quicker
to reject substandard entertainments.

Furthermore, Langdon inevitably faced difficulties adjusting to the film medium. Many years as a vaudeville comedian didn't necessarily prepare him for performing in front of a camera lens. Instead of the instantaneous feedback from a live audience, he had only the reaction of the crew to help him gauge a laugh.

Paradoxically, silent films were made in the noisiest of environments. The actors were forced to rely on their own concentration to tune out the sounds of hammers and saws. There was no "flashing red light" to indicate that filming had begun.

One of the most elusive adjustments for a film comedian is the realization that a gag that works with a live audience, or on the set, may not necessarily be funny on the screen. Woody Allen commented:

> If you're talking about a live audience, I'm right [in predicting comic effect] almost all of the time. But that has nothing to do with films and it makes you crazy.
> You know what to do and yet when you film it there is something that happens that casts a different perspective on it and sometimes it doesn't work when you see it. There are so many factors you're bucking. That's why films are so hard. [1]

Years of live performances couldn't prepare Harry for this. He had to start from scratch like all the others.

Simply put, Langdon was learning to cope with dozens of complex variables. It was an awkward period, but an essential stage of his growth. When later developments crowded upon him, Harry was familiar with some of the technical and artistic problems involved, and could perform for the camera with a measure of relaxation and assurance. Discouraging though they were, Langdon's early comedies provided vital training.

Sennett impatiently ordered his production chief, F. Richard Jones, to show the film of "Johnny's New Car" to every writer on the lot. Jones, a dedicated producer and an able writer/director (who later headed production at Roach) had supervised the new Langdon series. Like the early writers and directors, Jones had failed to find a handle for Harry.

Yet, he had faith in the boss's hunch. During one such
screening of the vaudeville film, a new gag man on the lot
was pressed into attendance. He was an intense young man
named Frank Capra.

Capra was born in Bisaquino, Sicily on May 18, 1897,
to an ignorant peasant couple whose children numbered seven.
He might have remained in Sicily but for his oldest brother,
who traveled to America and sent for his family several years
later. Young Capra spent his sixth birthday in the cramped
steerage hold of a steamship crossing the Atlantic. After
passing through immigration headquarters on Ellis Island,
the Capra family traveled by train to Los Angeles where they
made their home.

At a very young age, Capra became acutely aware of
the limitations caused by ignorance and illiteracy. He was
determined not to get caught in the same dead end that had
stymied his family and compatriots. In his autobiography,
The Name Above the Title, he wrote:

> I hated being poor. Hated being a peasant. Hated
> being a scrounging newskid trapped in the sleazy
> Sicilian ghetto of Los Angeles. I wanted out. A
> quick out. I looked for a device, a handle, a pole
> to catapult myself across the tracks from my scurvy
> habitat of nobodies to the affluent world of some-
> bodies.

Despite pressure from his peers, neighbors, and family,
Capra would not quit school after he had learned to read and
write.

In order to continue his education into high school and
college (he entered the California Institute of Technology in
1915), Capra worked at anything that became available, never
forgetting to give a large portion of his earnings to his humble parents. He played guitar in local bistros, worked as a
janitor, bucked rivets, waited tables, stuffed papers at the
Los Angeles Times, and still managed to stay at the head of
his class.

In 1918, Capra received a degree in Chemical Engi-
neering and could have landed a lucrative job (for the country
was then at war) but enlisted in the Army instead. After de-
mobilization, the post-war recession prevented him from finding employment in his chosen field. He became seriously ill

and depressed, and left home to drift from job to job, never far from broke.   He found occasional employment and eventually (out of desperation) talked his way into a job as the director of a one-reel film adaptation of Rudyard Kipling's FULTAH FISHER'S BOARDING HOUSE poem.

With no further opportunities behind the camera, 1922 saw Capra entering the film industry at a film processing laboratory, where he printed, dried, and spliced film.   His capacity for hard work and ability to learn eventually helped him land a job as a prop boy for Hollywood comedy director Robert Eddy.   Soon he became Eddy's film editor.   It was Eddy who introduced Capra to Robert McGowan, the director of Hal Roach's OUR GANG series.

As a gag man for OUR GANG, Capra demonstrated an innate facility for finding humor in everyday, down-to-earth situations, but his stay at Roach lasted only six months.   Will Rogers (then starring in a successful series of short comedies for Roach) had befriended him and put in a word with Sennett for the young gag man who wanted to move on.   In late 1924, Frank Capra found his way to Sennett's studio as a writer, not long after Langdon had arrived on the lot.

Despite all the lean times that Capra had experienced after his Army days, he remained essentially an optimist. In direct contrast to him was Arthur Ripley, an essentially pessimistic graduate of the New York film and theater world. Ripley, two years older than Capra, was a brooding intellectual with sunken eyes, a moustache, and stooped shoulders. He had been in the film business from the age of fourteen, when he worked as a film cutter for the fledgling New York-based Kalem studio.   He moved to Vitagraph in 1912 and eventually edited films for several other studios in the years that followed.   Writers at Sennett worked in pairs; Ripley, the veteran, took Capra on as his partner.

According to Capra, the vaudeville film was screened and Dick Jones asked for comments or suggestions.   A number of other writers begged off, muttering darkly and quickly exiting.   That left the three men alone in the screening room.

Ripley had failed to see much potential in Langdon. "What kind of magic could transmogrify that twirp?" he moaned.   "I suggest prayer because at the moment I think only God can help us with Langdon. "

Something Ripley had said caused Capra to perk up. "Wait a minute.   That could be it!   Only God can help an elf like Langdon.   God's his ally, see?   Harry conquers all with goodness. "

"But where's the comedy?" Jones asked.

"Where's the comedy in Chaplin?" Capra argued. "It's in his character, the Little Tramp.   Harry'll be the Little Elf.   Why don't you let Ripley and me kick it around?"

While Capra's account probably telescoped several discussions, it rings true.   The new Langdon team of Capra and Ripley was ready to give Langdon more than a tired formula. They had a concept.

NOTE

1.   Lax, Eric.   On Being Funny.   New York: Manor Books, Inc. , 1975, pp. 115-116.

Chapter Three: ACTOR AS AUTEUR

Capra and Ripley decided that Harry would portray the Eternal Innocent. Capra had been reading a book about Good Soldier Schweik, an Austrian soldier who left a path of goodness behind him. He felt that Harry might adapt some of that premise. His optimism would protect him against disaster. But how would that general concept be translated into screen action?

The new Langdon Unit (which also included director Harry Edwards) spent hours examining the early, ill-advised Langdon films. They scrutinized every frame for traces of something original or promising that could be expanded. To their surprise, they discovered one curious fact: when the frantic Sennett pace slowed for a moment, Harry showed traces of genuine pantomimic ability.

In PICKING PEACHES, Harry finds himself at a seaside beauty contest. He sits at a table watching the show, while flirting with a friendly young girl. For the first time, his mouth turns up at the edges into an impish "V"--later a trademark--and his eyes blink coyly. His sexual awareness suggests Chaplin, but Harry appears comfortable with the camera up close. His stiff movements of the slapstick scenes are superseded by a more natural, pliant manner.

Accordingly, Langdon was given a full-fledged comic monologue in closeup in his new film, THE LUCK OF THE FOOLISH (1924). His not-too-simple problem was to shave on a moving train. Langdon faces the camera and shaves over the shoulder of another traveler, who also faces forward.

The train is rocking, but that doesn't stop Harry from using
a dangerously sharp straight razor. His bland obliviousness
to the potential danger protects him, but drives the other guy
crazy. He can't stop watching Harry's reflection as Langdon
accomplishes a series of ridiculous finishing touches with
that razor, including a painful-looking corkscrew motion to
clear some lather out of his ear.

THE LUCK OF THE FOOLISH was an improvement,
but Harry had already unearthed the meek, put-upon personality (albeit erratically) in the earlier films. The difference
is strictly a matter of nuance. His I. Q. seems to have sunk
to a lower ebb; his childishness is a bit more obvious. Yet,
for no reason, a typical Sennett scene--a "hurricane" unleashed by an open door in a sleeper railroad car--is in-
serted, giving Langdon nothing better to do but stumble stu-
pidly around, falling over the other passengers. The proceedings are without form or structure.

The second interesting sequence has Harry handcuffed
to a hardened criminal. The juxtaposition of this dangerous,
animal-like killer and innocent Harry causes the viewer's attention to quicken. An interesting idea--evil and innocence
immutably joined. The promising idea remains undeveloped.
A stray bullet quickly sunders the connection.

THE LUCK O' THE FOOLISH is an uneasy mixture of
the old and the new, and makes no great impression. The
many elements that eventually comprised Langdon's developed
screen persona did not coalesce for six more comedies.
Even so, that is a remarkably short gestation period. Obviously, Langdon and his writers had their creative juices
flowing.

Writing for the Little Elf was not easy. While Langdon discovered his pantomimic vocabulary, Capra and Ripley
struggled with the problem of building gag sequences for him.
First, Langdon had to be funny. Where would they go for
the laughs? How would a helpless elf act? How could he
come to be involved in the necessary conflicts? A little guy
whose only ally was God couldn't act aggressively. That was
the main difference. He faced problems similar to those of
Lloyd, but instead of heroics, he would take the comical path
of least resistance.

Violence was the main idiom of silent comedy. How
else could conflict be externalized in a visual medium?

The instigation wasn't the problem. Harry could be treated violently, and often was. Wives screamed at him, bullets whizzed by him, vamps tried to kill him. He could attract trouble as honey attracts bees.

But what was the solution? Capra's plan prevented Harry from acting in his own behalf--responsibly. Harry would try to cope, always falling far short of success. Years later, Capra capsulized his rule which he dubbed the Principle of the Brick: "Langdon might be saved by the brick falling on the cop, but it was verboten that he in any way motivate the brick's fall. "

The writers realized that Harry would have to survive not by his own efforts but by trust alone. Thus, one of the bases of their concept was that Harry's universe would be (essentially) benevolent. Although trouble might close in on Harry, good would triumph in the end. Faith was all that was necessary to win--complete surrender. The meek shall inherit the earth wasn't Harry's motto, it was the story of his cinematic life.

Even as simple a thing as catching a football (in FEET OF MUD, 1924) could only be accomplished by faith. After running out for a pass, Langdon suddenly stops. He stands stock still, holding out his arms for the ball. Waiting patiently, trustingly. He may even have closed his eyes. Obediently, the ball comes straight to him. If he would have jockeyed for position under the ball in the normal way, it would certainly have eluded him.

The accident became his stock-in-trade. When Harry's girl is kidnapped in Chinatown (again in FEET OF MUD), Harry inadvertently stumbles into the secret entrance to her prison. He survives by sheer luck and escapes with the damsel by tumbling through a hidden trapdoor and sliding down a chute that deposits them on the sidewalk. Part of Harry's charm came from his acceptance of these phenomena in his boyish stride. He never doubted. He didn't have enough smarts.

Often his clumsy efforts boomeranged back at him with violent repercussions. The first portion of another short comedy from this period, BOOBS IN THE WOOD (1924), demonstrates one variation.

Harry, dressed in flannel and denim, aspires to

FEET OF MUD, with Natalie Kingston (Sennett/Pathe, 1924).
(The Museum of Modern Art, New York City)

become a lumberjack.   He finds himself in the backwoods,
standing next to an enormous tree, perhaps two feet in diameter at the base.   He spits enterprisingly on his hands (a
frequent Langdon procedure before attempting a major under-
taking), takes careful swing and ... the axe bounces off the
trunk, flying wildly from his hands.   Although shaken, Harry
tries again and again.   Each time, his well-planned swing
brings him a violent shock.

Given his excessively passive character, Little Harry's
encounters with women usually involved role-reversal.   When
Maric Astaire flirts with the featherweight lumberjack and
then moves closer for a kiss, an alarmed Harry raises his
axe for protection.   Sex was a continual source of bewilder-
ment and even fear for the Elf.   His naivete made him something of a cautious virgin.

Sexual burlesque was also a major theme of ALL
NIGHT LONG (1924), an early film under the aegis of the
Langdon Unit.   This two-reeler is set in the first World
War, with Harry finding himself a guest in the farmhouse
of a French peasant family.   The girl (Natalie Kingston)
somehow finds Harry irresistible.   (One of the vagaries of
Langdon's films was that beautiful women constantly fell for
him.   It amazed him as much as the audience.)

Natalie kisses Harry passionately.   When she finally
releases him from the embrace, Harry is in some form of
drugged stupor.   He falls backward (his body rigid) out an
open window.   Outside, he staggers about, nuzzling the farmhouse wall.   The kiss and the fall have left him doubly stunned.   In Harry's world, one very nearly always led to the
other.

Very soon, Harry Edwards and cameraman William
Williams began to take advantage of Langdon's odd physical
attributes.   His face in particular showed signs of becoming
something extraordinary.   Langdon had fat cheeks, jowls
actually, which usually created a moon-faced effect.   It was
essential that he be photographed mostly straight on, full
face.   In profile, he looked quite ordinary.

Harry had big pale eyes (blue), which may have looked
blank due to myopia.   He accented those eyes even further
by applying thicker than usual mascara.   To complete the
impish effect, his mouth was lipsticked into a modified, elon-
gated cupid's bow.   His mousey hair looked soft and fuzzy on

top. A Napoleonic curl frequently formed a comma in the
middle of his forehead, over eyebrows that tended to turn up
expectantly. He had dimples.

Langdon found that if he covered his face with light
make-up, almost clown-white, the babyface illusion was
heightened. The details of his cheekbones would wash out,
leading the viewer to his eyes, which became perhaps his
most important tool. A blink became a major screen event.

The emergence of Harry's eccentric appearance and
mannerisms occurred through incessant improvisation. He
was performing instinctively, never sure exactly what he
would do. While Williams was setting up the camera, Capra
and Ripley would explain the general situation of the scene
to be filmed. Langdon was given extraordinary latitude in
interpreting those instructions. As the emphasis moved from
the gags themselves to Harry's character, the humor was increasingly derived from his reactions (panic in slow motion)
to the unexpected. The actor himself became the focal point.

Edwards had persuaded Sennett to allow Capra and
Ripley on the set with him. The system was still freewheel-
ing enough that many good gags could originate during shooting. The writers' involvement in the creative evolution of
the Elf amounted to co-directorship.

In order to create the proper mood (and drown out the
din of the Sennett troops), musicians were brought onto the
set, again contrary to studio policy. Edwards would call for
action, and the comedian would go into his routine.

When Harry faltered in early comedies like THE SEA
SQUAWK (1924), bland scripting and tepid gags were usually
responsible. Even with Langdon in female drag--a potentially
hilarious idea--the results are flat. THE SEA SQUAWK may
be his worst Sennett two-reeler. Harry looks funny, like the
Pillsbury dough-boy in drag. But the story (some melodra-
matic nonsense about a jewel-smuggling ring) leaves Harry
very little to do. Capra's character fix is not apparent.

Even the better comedies from this period have serious shortcomings. BOOBS IN THE WOOD ends with Harry
as a sharp-shooter bouncer in a rough logging town tavern.
He has strings secretly attached to dozens of objects around
the room. If an object should fail to jump when Harry takes
aim and fires, the strings will make up for his errant bullets.

THE SEA SQUAWK, with Langdon on the right (Sennett/Pathe, 1925).   (The Museum of Modern Art, New York City)

But elaborate string gags were more a specialty of mechanical-minded Keaton, not dimwitted Harry.   For if Harry was bright enough to rig up those strings, he wouldn't need God as his ally.   Besides, a smart Harry just wasn't as amusing as a dumb one.

The second half of ALL NIGHT LONG is as clumsy as the first half is assured.   The film trades personality-oriented humor for a series of witless battlefield antics. (After an explosion, Harry is half-buried with his legs jutting out of the dirt at unlikely angles, nearly touching his ears. By the time Harry discovers that those legs belong to another man, it has long--too long--been obvious to the audience.)

Capra was wrong to claim that the change took place with
THE LUCK O' THE FOOLISH.   They stumbled more than
once.

*   *   *

Talent can be tapped, encouraged, even conjured.   The Langdon Unit did their best to find the kind of externals that would
stimulate Harry.   They worked hard to develop scripts that
would give Langdon the best springboard material possible.
But none of it would have mattered if the comedian's innate
talent hadn't risen to the occasion.

Without the security of an iron-clad vaudeville act,
Harry was working with a kind of unconscious abandon.   The
extraordinary results came from a combination of his vaudeville character, half-remembered bits from other periods in
his past, movements dictated by his pear-shaped body and
unique face, and a series of dream-like physical flourishes
that (seemingly) appeared out of nowhere.

In his excellent book The Silent Clowns, Walter Kerr
wrote: "The image that was arrived at ... cannot have been
entirely imposed.   Langdon, at maturity, is too deeply em-
bedded in what he does to have been directly instructed in
his unaccountable behavior."   Instead, Capra and company
stood on the sidelines, throwing in quick suggestions and
laughing when Langdon surprised them with an off-the-cuff
spurt of spontaneous whimsy.

Capra and Ripley understood that the characteristics
that made up the Elf's personality had to originate with the
comedian.   Instead of trying to force Langdon into a conceptual pattern, they tailored laughs and conflicts to showcase
his blossoming pantomimic skill.   Significantly, they were
taking their cues from the comedian.   In that sense, the
actor was the auteur, although not always directly or con-
sciously.   Harry had not been in films long enough to run
the whole show.

Langdon unquestionably benefited from strong guidance.
The Langdon Unit found the cinematic form that defined the
Elf's relationship with the world around him, and success-
fully provoked laughter from his childish ineptitude.   In short,
they insured that the films were funny.   More than that,
Capra's concept of a benevolent universe added meaning and

significance to Langdon's portrayal of a trusting innocent. The Sennett comedies had a unifying, optimistic theme that "said" something.

The camera caught and conveyed a whole that was greater than the sum of its parts. The result was one of the most dazzling collaborations in silent comedy. The Little Elf came to life.

Chapter Four: THE LITTLE ELF

The year 1924 had been one of charting a direction for
Harry's screen character. The early months of the following year represented a period of consolidation. Not until
PLAIN CLOTHES, released in the spring of 1925, was Langdon closer to the finished image of his later feature films
than to the ordinary comic of the first two-reelers.

REMEMBER WHEN? (1925) provides one of the most
satisfying narratives of his first period in "full bloom. "
Harry Hudson's childhood is economically established in the
opening segment. Six-year-old Harry must say goodbye to
a fellow orphan, young Rosemary Lee. (A rather woeful
looking boy stood in for Harry as a child, adding sincerity
and realism to the story.) Rosemary's new mother gives
Harry a locket with the girl's picture.

Grown-up Harry becomes a tramp as he wanders
through the countrysides and hobo-habitats, hoping to find
his childhood love. He wears a long, ankle-length coat and
carries a bindle stick. In the woods, he discovers a picnic
table laden with food. He is so overeager to eat that he
can't make up his mind where to start. Before he can bite
into one sandwich, he is distracted to another, then another.
His indecision gives the picnickers time to catch Harry hov-
ing over their food.

Harry resorts to stealing chickens. He opens his
coat, tosses a handful of feed inside, and the chicken oblig-
ingly jumps after the food. The Elf smiles, pleased with
his ingenuity, until he comes face-to-face with the irate

34

farmer. Harry's coat bulges ridiculously. When a chicken's head pops into view, the game is up, and Harry is quickly divested of his loot.

Seeking a quick escape, Harry joins "Mack's Circus Caravan," not suspecting that his childhood sweetheart (Natalie Kingston) is also aboard. When the circus sets up, Harry first unloads some heavy trunks (using Minerva the elephant as a chiropracter for his bent-over back), then helps pound some tent stakes. Suddenly, the Elf notices an incredible coincidence: the circus is setting up nearby the Hillcrest Orphanage, where he got his start in life. He smiles as the happy memories flood back. He pulls out the locket and kisses it. A quick kick in the pants from a co-worker brings Harry out of his daze.

Soon Harry meets Rosemary, but doesn't recognize her in her guise as the Bearded Lady. He is not sure how to act. At first he starts to tip his hat, then (taking notice of the beard) he offers her a cigar. After he agrees to deliver a note for her to the orphanage, Harry meekly touches her beard. He rubs his own bare chin, trying to comprehend the gender confusion. Scratching his forehead, a befuddled Harry leaves to run his errand.

Rosemary has also been looking for Harry. A note from the orphanage reveals his identity, and the lost lovers happily embrace. At that moment, the phoney beard falls off. Harry gently touches her face, then his own. With their search at an end, the film closes.

LUCKY STAR (1925) has none of the sweet nostalgia of REMEMBER WHEN?, but it also reaches into the comedian's show business past for story material. Instead of the circus, Langdon's time with turn-of-the-century traveling medicine shows is exploited. Perhaps as a result, Harry plays a more innocent young man than he had in REMEMBER WHEN?

Harry Lamb gazes dreamily at the heavens, looking for his lucky star. He optimistically sets off by train to find fame and fortune. Within minutes, a quick-talking con man, "Doc" Hiram Healy (Vernon Dent), fleeces the unsuspecting "lamb" of his savings. Harry becomes the Doc's assistant.

They arrive in the Mexican town of "San Tobasco,"

PLAIN CLOTHES, with Vernon Dent, who was the closest
Langdon came to having a regular partner (Sennett/Pathe,
1925).   (Michael Copner Collection)

where they set up the wagon.   Harry plays banjo and sings
to attract the crowd.   While the Doc makes his pitch, it is
Harry's job to circulate among the unruly crowd with the bot-
tles of elixir, collecting the money.

Señorita Mazda (Kingston) is the daughter of the town
pharmacist, whose business is threatened by Healey's tonic.
Her hot-blooded reaction is to get rid of them by any means
possible.   She hides a sharp dagger in her dress and lures
Harry Lamb to the slaughter.

She reclines seductively on her balcony, making bedroom eyes at the little guy.   Unexpectedly, Harry curls up
on her lap, resting his head against her breast like a baby.
Before she can use her weapon, the Elf is summoned back
to the wagon to mix up some more tonic.

Unbeknownst to Harry, the pharmacist tampers with
the formula.   The angry mob tars and feathers the Doc, and
Harry barely escapes the same fate.   He scampers out of
town, dodging gunfire and holding onto his hat.   The "lamb"
escaped unscathed, perhaps a bit wiser than before.

*   *   *

One of the last elements of Harry's comedy arsenal that jelled
was his costume, his "official duds. "   In his first efforts, he
dressed for whatever role he assumed: doughboy, football
player, street cleaner.   Just as his role varied, the image
he presented shifted from film to film.

By the time Langdon became the Little Elf, and no one
else, the Langdon Unit saw the need to give him one identifi-
able costume which, with a few variations, would remain constant.   The Little Tramp had proven the commercial advantage
of wearing essentially the same outfit in successive films.
Furthermore, the outfit was perfectly suited to his tramp-
clown image.   Langdon, too, needed a costume that would
compliment his babyish nature.

He took to wearing a felt hat with the brim turned up
all the way around.   It had a big dent on top, possibly a
symbol of his mental deficiencies.   He wore a tight double-
breasted coat with two rows of dollar-sized buttons.   It was
snug around his narrow shoulders and tended to flair out wide
at his waist.

He wore baggy pants and a pair of trusty slapshoes
(of comparatively normal size). The coat in particular had
a Little Lord Fauntleroy look that enhanced his boyish appearance. On several occasions, as in REMEMBER WHEN?,
he also donned a floor-length overcoat that dwarfed his di-
minutive frame still further.

The formulation of the "Langdon Look" coincided with
the precipitation of the Little Elf's persona. The Langdon
team had swept away most of the chaff, leaving only the elements that contributed to his portrait of a full-grown man
with the mind of a child. As his screen dimensions took
shape, audiences grew to enjoy and anticipate Harry's understated comedy style. The Little Elf became a viable, recognizable presence.

Confronted with the unknown, the Elf would invariably
blink slowly several times and try to make the best of things.
If good times came, he'd flip a little wave of welcome--tenta-
tively, though, since he'd been wrong before. Down on his
luck, he'd grow wistful beyond words, and rest a puffy cheek
on a stubby fist.

In a three-quarters shot (almost always from the left),
one cheek would puff way out if he set his jaw a certain way.
The cheek would grow and grow, as if someone was inflating
it with a bicycle pump. It made the bottom of his face look
soft and doughy. On an adult, those cheeks would come from
years of chewing tobacco. On Langdon, they helped form his
babyish pout.

Forever bewildered and confused, Harry stumbled
through life, constantly trying to make good. Critics have
observed that Harry was always imitating his betters, forever rehearsing for adulthood. Fortunately, dim-witted Harry
never had to pass an I. Q. test. If he had the mind of a
child, it was a child who flunked kindergarten. Who else
would try to hide while running across an open lawn by simply ducking his head?

In HIS MARRIAGE WOW (1925), he is late for his
wedding. When he finally arrives, the church entrance is
too crowded to permit him passage. He starts running along
the sidewalk to the backdoor. Midway he stops. He has noticed something--a window he might jump through. Too bad
it is at least ten feet over his head, made of stained-glass
and therefore welded shut. He jumps. His feet clear the

HIS MARRIAGE WOW, with Natalie Kingston (Sennett/Pathe, 1925). (The Museum of Modern Art, New York City)

sidewalk by all of six inches.   It is a pathetic attempt, but
Harry was always hopeful, even when the odds were stacked
against him.

To add to his perpetual confusion, Harry was constantly stunned by various sleep-inducers.   Often, a clunk
on the head (with a brick in FEET OF MUD) would do the
trick.   His eyes would mist over, his smile would flicker
momentarily and his legs would grow rubbery.   Sometimes
he would curl up on the floor in the fetal position.   He never
seemed very far from the womb.

In PLAIN CLOTHES, detective Harry opens a gas jet
in a wall to "gas out" the villains, but stands too close.
Gradually his eyelids grow heavier until he sinks senseless
to the floor.   The advent of slumber by many means was a
Langdon specialty.

Although his face and hands are generally considered
his best points, Langdon's footwork was astonishingly nimble
and completely individual.   Encountering an unusual object in
his path, he used a little sideskip to avoid trouble.   If an
enemy chased him around a table, and he couldn't decide to
break left or right, Harry would dance back and forth (his
arms and legs stiff), looking as if he was being pulled both
ways by unseen forces.

When angered (or pushed too far) he would pull his
hand up to his face, point an index finger and squint at the
enemy as if to say: "Now you better look out, buster!"   If
the foe yelled "BOO!" Harry's eyes would pop in shock, his
hands would fly to his hatbrim, and he'd run for cover.   His
coordination always evoked the awkwardness of a youth getting
used to his body.

"In a day when comics out-exaggerated each other,"
Capra wrote, "Langdon played scenes delicately, almost in
slow motion.   You could practically see the wheels of his
immature mind turning as it registered tiny pleasures or
discomforts."[1]

His acting style conveyed the external equivalent of
shifting psychological impulses.   He was like a weather vane,
yielding to the prevailing winds, navigating through the per-
plexing events that swirled around him.

Fortunately, he looked light, with faster-than-normal

silent speed working in his favor.   One felt he would bob to
the surface before serious undertows could take hold.

Small, kid-sized objects proliferated.   Although he
could drive a car, he preferred to ride a bike or walk.   If
he wrote a love letter, he stuffed it into a tiny envelope.
In PLAIN CLOTHES, Langdon pulls out a gun that looks like
a cap pistol.

Yet, Harry occasionally reminded the viewer that the
Elf also had a bit of the adult in him.   In HIS MARRIAGE
WOW his relationship with Natalie seems basically normal.
The Elf held any number of jobs from foundry worker to
fireman.

Walter Kerr speculated: "What I think won Langdon
his first audience and held it transfixed for a time, was ...
a complexity so dense and unfathomable that it pushed silent
screen fantasy to its farthest limits.   It was his status as
something that could not be, but was, that gave his audiences
its first, greatest pleasure. "[2]

In a sense, the Elf was a denizen from another dimension, not of this earth, yet trapped here among mere mortals.   He illuminated human faults and foibles from a special
perspective, like Swift's Gulliver or Twain's Huck Finn.   Little Harry was a stranger in a strange land, reflecting the essential absurdity of our culture, our mores, and our very
existence.

*   *   *

Langdon's career in silent comedy shorts was greatly enhanced by some excellent supporting players.   He had his
pick of the Sennett stock company including leading talents
like Madeline Hurlock and Andy Clyde, both stars in their
own right.   A vivacious brunette named Natalie Kingston
deftly played his girl, or the vamp, in a handful of the best
two-reelers.

Vernon Dent contributed the best support.   Dent was
an all-purpose straight man and villain for several lesser
silent comics.   Few straight men had his ability to completely submerge themselves in such a wide variety of comic
foils.

Within this first partnership with Harry (they were to

team up again, years later), Vernon Dent played a football
coach, a music instructor, a girl-chasing buddy, a prime
minister, an escaped lunatic, and a sergeant.   He donned
an incredible assortment of wigs, moustaches and costumes.
His only really consistent feature was his powerful, beefy
frame.

Dent was the closest thing to a regular partner Harry
Langdon ever had.   Dent's characters represented the usually
harsh realities of the world that always made things tough for
the Elf.   Their comic rhythm together is so remarkable that
it occasionally resembles that of Laurel and Hardy.   Harry
and Vernon were so well-matched that it is difficult to shake
the notion that they could have made an extraordinary team,
if that had been in the cards.

Two scenes from HIS MARRIAGE WOW demonstrate
the crazy heights they could achieve together.   Dent plays
Professor McGlumm ("Student of Melancholia and Pessimism"),
who is trying to convince Harry that his new wife wants to
poison him for an insurance policy.   Every time Harry tries
to take a sip of wine or coffee, he catches McGlumm's bale-
ful eye and stops short.   Then Harry looks fondly at his
pretty bride and, reassured, tries again.   The emotional
undercurrents flow between Langdon and Dent like a kind of
psychological ballet of doubt, warning, and reassurance.
Each shake of Dent's head and insecure smile on Langdon's
lips is timed so perfectly that they seem to operate as one.

The second remarkable episode is a wild car chase.
By this time, the viewer (but not Harry) has discovered that
McGlumm is actually an escaped lunatic.   When he takes the
wheel of Harry's car to outrace the asylum van, Harry goes
berserk at McGlumm's crazy driving.   As they career crazily
through busy intersections, McGlumm informs Harry that he
is really Barney Google.

Comprehension finally having dawned on Harry, he tries
to grab the wheel, so McGlumm yanks it off the steering col-
umn, tossing it high into the air.   He cackles insanely as
Harry shrinks back in terror while the vehicle speeds out of
control.   It is a broad, slapstick situation, but so individual
are its participants that it seems totally fresh.

Even though the primary focus on Harry precluded
them from becoming a genuine team, Dent's contribution to

Langdon's films is incalculable. Yes, Harry could have done
with other straight men, and did, but not one was as much
fun, or as brilliant a collaborator, as Vernon Dent.

NOTES

1. Capra, Frank. The Name Above the Title. New York:
   The Macmillian Company, 1971, p. 62.
2. Kerr, Walter. The Silent Clowns. New York: Alfred
   A. Knopf, 1975, p. 267.

Langdon had great commercial and artistic success at the end of his time in Edendale.   In just eighteen months, Harry was acclaimed as the top comic of the two-reelers.   Sennett rewarded him with bigger budgets and added breathing room in a format sometimes called the "mini-feature."

SOLDIER MAN (1926) gives Harry an extra ten minutes (one reel) to develop the story more fully, yet avoid the risks involved in attempting a full-length feature.   In many ways, thirty minutes is an ideal length for Harry's unprepossessing character.   The shorter form occasionally limited the full realization of promising material.

In REMEMBER WHEN? Harry (for the first time) explores a circus milieu, certainly a setting rich in comic potential.   With only two reels, time constraints precluded all but a gag sequence with the elephant and the routine with the Bearded Lady.   One more reel would have given Capra and Ripley just enough time to investigate a few more aspects of the carnival world.

SOLDIER MAN divides neatly into two halves: Harry as a doughboy in Europe, and Harry as a substitute King. The film opens on Armistice Day, but no one had bothered to tell prisoner-of-war Langdon why he was set free.   The Elf wanders aimlessly through the barren hills.   He thinks the war is still on.   Finally he hears what sounds like combat.

It is a farmer blowing up stumps.   The farmer lights a

long fuse and runs for cover. Harry unknowingly snags the
dynamite with the barrel of his broken rifle. While chasing
the frightened farmer, Harry crawls through the dirt. Soon
he is huddled behind a cow for protection. His eyes keep
returning to the cow's udder. He is fascinated by the strange
apparatus. Harry gingerly fingers one or two of the nipples.
Then he sees the dynamite.

While Harry panics, the farmer spirits the explosives
away. The Elf thinks the cow has eaten the dynamite. He
orders the animal to spit it out. Listening at the cow's side
reveals nothing. Harry can only close his eyes.

When the explosion does come, the cow bolts. Harry
mistakes falling debris (the remains of a picnic lunch) for
bits of the unfortunate animal. He examines a few small
bones queasily.

In a nearby royal palace, drunken King Strudel of Bo-
mania (Langdon in a double role) is about to be kidnapped.
Within minutes, doughboy Harry (the exact double of the King,
of course) has been dressed in the sumptuous royal garments
for a big entrance before the court. Langdon wavers in a
back archway, having seen a tempting bowl of apples. He
takes bites from several, while the good Prime Minister
(trying to protect the throne) attempts to straighten Harry's
robes.

When Harry makes his entrance, he wonders aloud why
everyone is stooped over. Are they sick? He places his
crown on the floor beneath one man's head, hoping to avoid
a mess. On the throne, he rocks back and forth like a child.
He knows nothing of royal protocol, stepping down from the
throne to ask his Prime Minister a humble question. When
the evil Duke calls him an imposter, Harry orders the man
decapitated. He's having a ball playing King!

Later, in the Queen's royal bedchamber, the Elf is
blissfully unaware that she is plotting revenge for his drunken
insults. She will stab him when he kisses her. But Harry
is frankly more interested in a tray full of tiny sandwiches
and pieces of toast. He excuses himself from the clutch several times for return trips to the snack tray.

They finally embrace. Her hand raises up with the
knife, but gradually goes limp. The knife falls to the floor,
along with the Queen. The Elf has unexpected sexual power.

Again they kiss, again she faints. Observing the body of the
Queen on the floor, Harry decides that making love is ex-
huasting work. He lays down on the royal bed and instantly
falls asleep.

Suddenly the Queen is shaking him, waking him. The
"Queen" turns out to be Harry's wife. He has been dream-
ing from the start. That last part wasn't so bad, Harry remembers. He kisses his wife just as he had kissed the
"Queen" ... but nothing happens. She does not collapse onto
the cushion Harry has considerately placed beneath her. As
his wife stares at him in disbelief, the film ends.

Probably the most memorable part of SOLDIER MAN
is the elaborate throne room set. Sennett gave his star surprisingly lavish surroundings for a short comedy. But a
hard critical eye at the scenario indicates that the story could
have used a bit more attention. The doughboy sequences lack
gags tailored for Langdon. Later, most of the laughs in the
palace come from business obviously improvised on the set.
Only Langdon's usual immersion in his character, and reliable comic impulses and reactions, elevate SOLDIER MAN to
a successful entertainment. It was a big box-office hit.

In SATURDAY AFTERNOON (1926), probably the greatest
of Langdon's Sennett comedies, Harry's opening title quickly
pinpoints his role: "Harry Higgins, just a crumb from the
sponge cake of life." He is a foundry worker, eagerly waiting for the noon whistle to signal his freedom on a short
Saturday workday. When the whistle finally blows (he has
nearly burned himself twice on red hot metal), the crush to
board the street car finds him impotently pushing on the
crowd in a doomed attempt to catch a ride.

For a moment, he stops to ponder his dilemma, blinking owlishly. He remembers that he must call his wife.
Harry runs to a nearby phone booth. His angry wife (Alice
Ward) berates him for his stupidity in missing the car.
Harry's facial expression grows exceedingly wistful. He
holds the receiver at arm's length. Although her tirade is
not over, he sets the receiver down and leaves the booth altogether.

Enter Steve Smith (Vernon Dent) who beckons Harry.
Steve is making time with two "heartbreakers" and tells a
dubious Harry "the one with the swell lamps is dying to
meet you!" Harry awkwardly shakes her hand, nodding,

Sennett never let the public forget that Langdon was the
latest in his series of major discoveries (ca. 1924).
(Academy Collection)

and makes to run off, but Steve insists that Harry walk with
one of the girls.

As Harry and the girl walk along a sidewalk, she impulsively grabs his hand.   He swings her arm like a five-
year-old, smiling sweetly.   She tries to carry his lunch box
for him, but Harry childishly won't let it go.   When the girl
accidentally pulls down the strap of his overalls, his reaction
is one of absolute alarm.   Will she strip him right on the
street?   He seems to think so.

Returning home can't be one of the Elf's favorite ex-
periences.   His wife's welcome is deadly.   As Harry enters
and sits humbly in a wooden chair near the door, his wife
glares angrily at him, her arms folded.   Earlier she discovered that he has "wasted money" buying a pack of cigar-
ettes.

Harry tries to make up.   He offers to shake her hand.
When that fails, he offers her the weekly pay envelope, but
that only buys him a temporary truce.   She must leave the
room to put the money away.

Now Harry takes the opportunity to tell her off--after
she is safely out of earshot.   (He even takes care to lock
the door.)   "From now on, I'm going to be the boss!" he
declares, gaining confidence and bearing as he takes a few
strutting steps and draws himself up.   "After this, you're
gonna wind the clock, fix the cat and poison the ants--!"
What Harry fails to notice is that his wife has entered the
room through the other door and stands about three feet behind him.

"You're not the only woman," he continues, really getting worked up.   "I've got a date with a pair of beautiful
lamps!"   He stomps his foot.   When she reveals her presence, however, his epochal anger deflates into a series of
insecure, apologetic gestures.   To call his bluff, she hands
him a dime which, she says, he'll need on his date.

At 2:00 p.m., Harry slides out a back window, dressed
in his best suit, and he and Steve hop in a car to meet their
dates.   They are running a bit late; when no one is waiting
in front of the corner candy store, Steve blames Harry, la-
menting: "You don't find nice girls like them every day."

Harry looks around and disappears behind a corner.

Moments later, he struts into view with two sexy blonds, one
on each arm. Harry gives the girls a series of sideways
winks, and presents them to Steve.

His friend is unimpressed. He whispers: "They won't
do."

Automatically, Harry turns to the girls and announces:
"You won't do!" Insulted, the girls turn out to be rough and
attack Steve. Harry throws a brick to protect his friend.
The store window shatters. Steve has to jump in his car to
catch up with Harry, who has run into the original "heartbreakers." The date is on after all.

Steve and the girls pile in the front seat, leaving the
rumble seat outside for Harry. He waves happily to the
riders in the cab through the back window. He even blows
a few awkward kisses.

To hide from his wife (driving the car in the adjacent
lane) Harry ducks down and closes the rumble seat. Steve
also recognizes Harry's wife and turns abruptly into a bumpy
field that adjoins the road. The ride is rough, and by the
time they coast to a stop and get out of the car, Steve thinks
he has thrown his friend off somewhere. He sends the girls
looking for Harry, but hears Harry's cries for help before
long. He opens up the rumble seat and pulls a stunned, be-
draggled Harry up into the open air. He falls headfirst over
the rear fender like a limp doll. Steve hoists Harry (whose
legs are wobbly) onto his feet, removing tools that have
lodged in his torn suit. Harry pushes away Steve's hands
and sinks forlornly to the running board.

Trouble is brewing elsewhere for Steve and Harry.
The two girls run into their boyfriends. The guys (who look
like hoodlums) decide to teach the usurpers a lesson. Steve
steps up to the toughs, while Harry hangs safely behind on
the running board, urging his friend on.

Harry makes a fist, swings, and nicks the end of his
nose. His cheeks quiver from the slight blow and he sinks
lower on his seat. As he pulls his tattered coat tighter
around him, looking wistfully withdrawn, he presents the
quintessential Harry Langdon image.

When Steve falls at Harry's feet, he points a finger:
"I'm disappointed in you, Steve!" And hands him a hammer.

Naturally, when Steve hauls back to launch the blow, the hammer head flies backwards and ricochets off Harry's dome.

Things look bad for Steve, so one of the girls fetches some "water" in hopes of reviving Harry. The water is really gasoline. One sip, and the Elf is on his feet, throwing a few scrappy punches into the air. He gamely enters the fray.

A quick blow to Harry's glass jaw causes his legs to buckle. Harry crawls away (passing right through the villain's legs). Seeking refuge, and again (as always) in a considerable mental fog, Harry crawls between the two cars that are parked together.

Within seconds, Harry faces a very strange predicament. He is sitting on one running board, and his feet are resting on the other, while both cars speed down a highway. His reaction--incredibly--is to curl up for a nap. The chase ends when a telephone pole comes between the cars, leaving Harry wrapped around it, suspended about three feet off the ground.

In the denouement, Harry's wife drives up. Seeing her Harry in bad shape, she bundles him into her car, and apologizes: "It's all my fault--I should never have given you that dime!" Harry is not sure how to take her apology at first. Then his dubious expression gives way to a weak smile. He lays his head on her shoulder and the (apparently) reconciled couple drive off together.

Despite some elements of run-of-the-mill slapstick comedy, SATURDAY AFTERNOON transcends banality through its ebullient mood and the skillful pantomime of the star. The narrative is complete, with a prologue (the factory), a beginning (his domestic conflict), a middle that develops (from the candy store to the open field), a climax (the fight), a big topper (the telephone pole) and a conclusion (the reconciliation). The supporting characters are quickly sketched, but solid and believable.

Most importantly, the plot and people provide a framework for Harry to work his magic. He performs most of his recognizable routines without seeming to throw them in arbitrarily. All is worked out in an orderly, enjoyable fashion.

The playful, energetic mood of SATURDAY AFTERNOON contrasts sharply with the dark mood of the following film, his last for Sennett. Although a return to the regular two-reel length, FIDDLESTICKS (1926) is nearly as good as the previous film. The mood most likely derives from pessimistic Arthur Ripley rather than up-beat Frank Capra.

Harry Hogan is an aspiring musician who has struggled valiantly under the tutelage of Professor Von Tempo (Vernon Dent). He yearns to play the bass fiddle, but fails ... miserably. Von Tempo gives him a diploma just to get rid of him.

Harry returns home full of excitement about his graduation. He enters the Hogan living room, sets down his fiddle, pulls out his diploma, and shows it to his father, who is reading a newspaper. "Look!--I'm a naturalized musician!" His father turns a page.

Harry takes a half step over to his brother and holds out the diploma. His brother crosses his legs and concentrates harder on his reading. From the left a second brother enters, fixing his tie. Harry does a double-take, then points (again) to his diploma. Rejected again, Harry's hands open palms up in a mild appeal.

His father rises, strides to the door, opens it and points outside. "Get out!--Before I remember I'm your father!"

Harry slowly kisses his mother goodbye, patting her on the arm. After Harry passes through the door, he sets the fiddle down, turns, and (with a cut to a medium two-shot) shakes a finger at his father. "All right for you!" Harry exclaims. His father slams the door.

Soon the camera is tracking behind Harry as he walks down the city sidewalk the next day. (He has spent the night in a bug-ridden room.) Suddenly he does a little sideways run and fingers a spot on his leg where a lingering bedbug bites.

The same thing happens again. He stops walking now, raises an arm (locked at the elbow, like a semaphore) and brings his hand down hard on the spot. He shakes his leg to let the smashed bug fall out. When it does, he skips to one side, a foot farther away.

Now he brings a leg (also straight) up high, then down in a blow that surely would have decimated the offending insect. But Harry has to make sure. He grinds it into the pavement under his well-worn sole. He bends over to look at it for a long time, then stomps the bug again. Harry, forever imitating his elders, has echoed the excessive brutality of his father.

The world of FIDDLESTICKS is a more hostile place. Penniless, the Elf tries to join Professor Von Tempo's street band. The second he places his bow to the strings and begins sawing away again, the falling nickels and dimes from appreciative city dwellers turn to brickbats. Harry (and his fiddle) are kicked unceremoniously out of the band. The Professor tears up his diploma.

All is not lost. Penrod the Junkman (Sennett's stereotypical Jew) quickly discovers that Harry has real talent for coaxing valuable junk from people's windows, his playing is that bad. They form a partnership, and even build a big chickenwire cage to protect him from falling debris.

Pleased with himself, Harry declares: "There's lots of money in music!"

Penrod agrees: "You got natural talent, kid."

Chapter Six: THE NEW BOSS

The summer of 1925 marked Harry Langdon's passage from hot newcomer to bona fide film star. The signs were unmistakable: everywhere, doors were opening for him.

On the set, the crew laughed long and hard at his every gesture. In restaurants, the diners buzzed with recognition when Harry entered the room, and they quickly queued up for autographs. Outside his Edendale dressing room, reporters and photographers jostled for an interview or exclusive photo. Langdon was forced to hire William H. Jenner as a personal manager to sort through the proliferating demands for his time.

His fan mail doubled, then doubled again. Reporter Jean North was a little awestruck when she ran into Harry in the studio of a prominent Hollywood portrait photographer. Langdon had just placed an order for $2000 worth of portraits which would be transported to the Sennett lot by truck.

The bottom line was that Langdon's presence on theater screens across the country (and in Europe, too) meant happy, laughing patrons and serious money at the box-office. His name was often billed on the marquis above the dramatic feature. Even the most cynical, jaded exhibitor could understand that there was real money to be made from the antics of the Little Elf.

Langdon was Sennett's top property. His salary increased (in a series of contractual revisions) from $250 a week to a staggering $7500 a week. During his last year in Edendale, Harry earned over a quarter of a million dollars.

Then the offers began to roll in. Mack Sennett had
known it would happen.   Langdon wanted to get out from
under Sennett's thumb and form his own production company.
He instructed Bill Jenner and Jerry Geisler (his attorney)
to sort through the offers.   Harry finally selected a bid from
John McCormick, a high ranking executive with First National
Pictures.   The contracts were signed on September 16, 1925.
Oddly enough, the man who signed on behalf of the film company was Sol Lesser, the independent producer who had discovered Langdon for films back in 1923.

First National was different from most conventional
studios.   It was an organization of exhibitors who owned
first-run theaters in thirty to thirty-five key cities, plus
many second-run houses.   First National avoided astronom-
ical film rental fees by forming partnerships with certain
stars and putting up the production money in advance.   The
performers would rent studio space, hire a staff, and super-
vise their own work.   Chaplin had signed with First National
in 1917, and Pickford a year later.   The concept proved successful.

In October, Harry Langdon moved into new headquarters on the United Lot in Burbank, the site where his early
comedies for Principal Pictures had been planned.   He took
his entire brain trust with him.

Harry Edwards had agreed to direct the first feature
only if Frank Capra and Arthur Ripley were also brought
over.   Harry, certainly in an expansive mood (and liking both
men), readily agreed.   All received substantial salary in-
creases.   Capra, by his own account, went from $75 to
$300 a week, then a handsome wage.

Langdon could afford it.   As president of the newly-
formed Harry Langdon Corporation, he stood to make a lot of
money.   The terms of the contract required him to deliver a
minimum of three feature films at a budget of $150,000 each
("A" pictures), with an option for three more at the same budget.
All told, First National would eventually put up a total of
$1,000,000 plus $6000 a week salary for the comedian, plus
25 percent of the profits.   (One source estimated that Harry's
share of the profits would net him anywhere from $60,000 to
$70,000 extra per picture.)   Salary for the director, writing
staff, co-stars and crew would be derived from the budget.   The
contract stipulated that the films would be made within a two-
year period, with production slated to begin on November 15, 1925.

Aside from matters of budget and salary, the big change was the man in charge. Instead of Mack Sennett, it was now Harry himself. He was the new boss, having complete creative control of his work. This had initially been a sticking point in negotiations. Despite Langdon's impressive track record, First National was reluctant to surrender all creative control. But such was their desire to sign him that they finally surrendered that point, with the understanding that Harry would confer with McCormick regarding the general plots of upcoming projects.

Part of the success of First National's artist-oriented arrangements was the stars they signed. Both Chaplin and Pickford proved to be canny (if occasionally troublesome) producers. But at this stage in his career, Harry Langdon could have been no one's idea of a production chief.

Gertrude Astor, soon to be Harry's co-star, created this portrait of Langdon in The Films of Frank Capra: "Harry Langdon was a funny little wordless man. He would never sit near anyone on the set; indeed, he would wander a block away and sit alone on a bench until Frank Capra needed him for a scene. Although a star, he acted like a non-entity."

One day, noticing Harry sitting off by himself, her curiosity caused her to investigate. "Why do you sit over here alone?" she asked.

He looked up at her and replied quietly: "Oh, I like it. I don't like people. I like to be alone and think."

"It was a contrast," Miss Astor remembered. "Frank Capra, so young and so serious, and Harry looking at you, blinking those pale blue eyes, and then glancing over his shoulder to make sure you weren't following him into his private world of silence."

Harry was extremely fortunate to be able to reassemble most of the original Langdon Unit in Burbank. Although he had the major voice in story ideas and worked closely with the writers, he delegated many of the more mundane production duties to Frank Capra and Arthur Ripley.

Capra was more than willing to step into the breach. He was eager to learn about every phase of the motion picture business. He had been straitjacketed at the Sennett studio by the limited participation allowed a gag man. He was fascinated by all the elements that formed a coherent cine-

matic expression and wanted to be familiar with them for
future reference. A lifelong champion of the "little guy,"
Capra was far from an elitest in his dealings with gaffers,
prop men, extras and the rest of the crew.

Langdon scored a major coup by signing veteran cameraman Elgin Lessley. Lessley was reckoned to be the best
comedy cameraman in the business, and was noted for his
knack of getting tricky shots with a minimum of fuss. He
had worked for Buster Keaton for years, having cranked the
camera for such innovative classics as THE PLAYHOUSE,
OUR HOSPITALITY, and SHERLOCK, JR.

Ripley, now officially head writer, assembled a first-
rate staff of gag men. Hal Conklin (a Sennett veteran), Murray
Roth, J. Frank Holliday, Tim Whelan, and Gerald Duffy
formed the team. Whelan and Duffy had both worked for
Harold Lloyd and would lend their experience in creating
feature-length scenarios. Counting Ripley, Capra, Edwards,
and Langdon, the Unit boasted nine experienced gag men.
All would be pushed to their creative limits, as they faced
the considerable task of constructing a full-length story for
the Little Elf.

Sennett had tested the feature comedy as early as
1915, with TILLIE'S PUNCTURED ROMANCE (starring Marie
Dressler, Mabel Normand and Charlie Chaplin), but the film's
length was largely a gimmick. It wasn't until the top screen
clowns began to feel constricted by the twenty-minute barrier
that comedies spilled over to three and four reels. When
Harold Lloyd began A SAILOR-MADE MAN (1921), he had envisioned it as a typical two-reeler. By the time he was done,
he had a film twice that length. The story had been too good
to edit down.

Beyond creative restrictions, the two-reeler was becoming economically unattractive to the major stars. Basically, production costs threatened to overtake expected income. One reason Chaplin had achieved his vaunted position
was his perfectionism, which drove budgets through the ceiling. Features offered the Tramp much more financial latitude.

In 1920, Buster Keaton starred in the feature-length
film, THE SAPHEAD. But as he had not written or directed
the film himself, it is not often considered the breakthrough
film. That honor has traditionally belonged to THE KID
(1921). After the Tramp proved that it could work, Keaton
and Lloyd quickly followed suit.

TRAMP, TRAMP, TRAMP, with Alec B. Francis (First National, 1926). (The Museum of Modern Art, New York City)

Comedy proved more difficult than drama to extend. Beyond a certain limit, the pitfalls became enormous. "Pacing is always a problem," Woody Allen recently observed. "Even the greatest [comedies] have langeur in them. There's no way out. There are moments that you tolerate. Once in a while you hit on something like DUCK SOUP that has practically no dead spot in it."[1]

Langdon took the other side of this debate. He felt a comedy could have too many laughs. "There should be a breathing spell between laughs, with a gradual development leading up to a laugh. A picture that is one laugh from start to finish becomes tedious. Relief is necessary."[2]

Langdon's late entry to feature-length comedy (five
years after THE KID) meant that he was entering the major
leagues. Now that he was bidding farewell to his association
with Sennett's knockabout farce, his work would (inevitably)
be measured against that of the reigning comedy kings. Could
he successfully make the transition?

His success in features was by no means a foregone
conclusion. The public had accepted the Little Elf as a sort
of comical flea who flitted through ludicrous short fantasies
and somehow survived. Would they accept him as the pro-
tagonist of longer, more involved stories? Even more crucial, would they pay to see Langdon alone, rather than in
support of another film? Until they did, no one could say
for sure.

The problem fell directly into the lap of Ripley's writing staff. They had to construct a story involving passive
Little Harry in the currents of plot intrigue and jeopardy,
providing believable excuses for Langdon to invoke his complex lexicon of gestures and perfected routines. If it took a
clever writer to plot a successful Langdon short, it would
require nothing short of brilliance to float Harry through a
film three times that length without becoming repetitious or
predictable.

The finished screenplay that became TRAMP, TRAMP,
TRAMP (1926) costarred Langdon with a San Antonio-born
dancer who had recently changed her name from Lucille
LeSuer to Joan Crawford. During her first two years in pictures, Crawford had been little more than a big-eyed ingenue
who won Charleston contests in her spare time. She wouldn't
become box-office for another two years, but had already supported Jackie Coogan and Constance Bennett. TRAMP, TRAMP,
TRAMP was to be her only loan-out from M-G-M in nearly
two dozen silent films.

Harry plays Harry Logan, the only son of an invalid
cobbler (Alec B. Francis) whose rent is overdue. It seems
that the big manufacturer of shoes in town is Burton Shoes
(for this tale begins in "Burton," Massachusetts), and they
are forcing the small-time shoemakers out of business.

Burton Shoes has hit on the publicity gimmick of spon-
soring a coast-to-coast walkathon with the prize of $25,000
to the winner. On the day before the race, huge crowds
gather to greet the racers. As the entrants are individually

Posed still of Harry on location for TRAMP, TRAMP, TRAMP
(First National, 1926). (The Museum of Modern Art, New York
City)

introduced, the crowd cheers them loudly. Mr. Burton watches,
beaming happily.

     The World Champion is announced. The crowd hushes
in expectation, craning their necks to catch his arrival. Suddenly, a lost-looking Harry toddles into view. The crowd
roars its welcome. He is startled. He looks around, scratching
his head, wondering why they are cheering. Then they close
in to shake his hand and wish him luck, causing him to become even more bewildered. Gradually, however, his expression changes. A little V-shapes smile flickers on his
lips as he gives in and accepts their good wishes.

     What can he be thinking? That this huge crowd, gath-
ered for the race, just happens to like his looks? That perhaps a life that has been quite unspectacular has suddenly
changed for the better? Or is it something much simpler:

surrendering to the predominant mood, never mind its inexplicable origins.   Why resist, when everyone seems to like you so much?

When the crowd greets the real champion instead, realizing their mistake, they abandon Harry. He stands alone, as quickly forgotten as he had been cheered. He blinks several times. His very figure radiates pathos. The viewer sees Harry's true relationship to society. He is an outcast.

Shaken, not sure what to do, Harry wanders over to a large billboard on the picnic grounds. The face that adorns the 24-sheet advertisement is Burton's daughter, Betty (Crawford). The billboards dot the countryside, and Harry has become smitten with the girl's picture. She is his fantasy love. Earlier he has declared: "I'm so crazy about her, I'm crazy."

Betty has watched Harry's rejection by the crowd and feels sorry for him. She crosses the grounds and stands behind Harry, who is still wistfully admiring the advertisement. Eventually, he sees her.

At first, Harry reacts ultra-slow, gradually making the connection between the real girl and the picture. The shock is almost too much. He is, by turns, delighted, afraid, bashful, and excited. He sits by her side, then pops up and retreats behind a nearby tree.

It is an extended, yet remarkable sequence. As James Agee observed: "Langdon showed how little ... one might use and still be a great silent-screen comedian."[3] The fact that this episode is remembered as one of his most characteristic proves that he could succeed with this type of rather thin material.

Joan Crawford thought so. She found Harry so funny that she couldn't stop laughing. Even after spoiling take after take, and apologizing for her unprofessional conduct, she would catch one glimpse of Harry's comical business and collapse into hysterics. Eventually, Edwards had her face away from the camera and close her eyes. Their two-shots were filmed later.

Betty convinces Harry to enter the race (the $25,000 providing the needed impetus). Before long, he is separated from the others and tries to take a short cut. After making his way through a flock of sheep on a hillside, Harry climbs

over a fence marked "No Trespassing." On the other side,
his sweater catches on a nail. He hasn't seen that there is
no ground beneath his feet; he is suspended over a sheer
drop of several hundred feet. Harry begins to pull his
sweater loose from the interfering nail. Later Langdon
wrote:

> Every man in a comedy company dreads to make
> thrill scenes. So often a man's life hangs on a
> bit of invisible wire, or his ability to conquer the
> instinctive fear of danger.
>   During the filming of TRAMP, TRAMP, TRAMP,
> nobody in the company wanted me to hang on a fence
> at the edge of a steep cliff. There was no one else
> to do it, so I had no alternative. You can be quite
> sure there was not a laugh in the crowd back of the
> camera while this stunt was being done.
>   When I got off the fence, I met nothing but
> blanched faces and silence, [he said. But when
> the episode played on the screen, audiences howled,
> causing Langdon to conclude:] The enjoyment of
> comedy, just like the enjoyment of tragedy, is the
> result of the feeling of remoteness from the situa-
> tion caricatured. [4]

Unfortunately, Harry's cliff-hanger was resolved by
cheating. When he finally does fall, he takes a whole section of the fence with him. He rides down the hill using the
fence as an improvised sled, dodging falling rocks. Where
was that hill just seconds before? The writers had written
themselves into a corner. The solution was a disappointment.

The cyclone climax, which may have inspired Keaton's
similar storm in STEAMBOAT BILL JR. (two years later),
presents one of the most absurd images of the film: the big,
strong champion cowering on his knees, hysterically begging
the Elf to save him.

Surprisingly, Harry saves the day in triumphant fashion. He chases the twister, throwing rocks--small pebbles--
into its maw. Abruptly, the cyclone turns and flees. The
title: "David slew Goliath, Joshua stopped the sun, Daniel
tamed the lions, but Harry Logan made a cyclone take the
air."

Harry's crush on Betty leads, improbably, to the altar.
They are now rich ($25,000 went a lot farther in 1926) and
... they have a child.

Betty: "I think I hear Harry Jr. crying."

Cut to Langdon himself, in an oversized rocking cradle, wearing a baby bonnet and holding a bottle! He chews at a teddy bear and gnaws on the side of his cradle. He tries to get a grotesquely long nipple on his formula bottle into his mouth, but it swings this way and that, too fast for Baby Harry's reactions.

He throws a ball which bounces back, caroming off his head. For the finish, he begins rocking back and forth and soon flips the cradle a complete 360 degrees. With that stunt, causing Harry's eyes to widen impossibly, the film ends.

The basic conflict of TRAMP, TRAMP, TRAMP surely originated with Frank Capra. His ethic was fundamentally derived from the biblical story of David and Goliath: the little guy, through pluck and perseverance, would inevitably conquer the complacent giant. Capra also believed deeply in the democratic ideals of his new homeland. Depression-era audiences responded strongly to Capra's later films based on these themes, and the power of his message added meaning to the struggles of Harry Logan.

Harry and his father work in a tiny store (probably living in the back), preferring to preserve their ideal of individual craftsmanship rather than submit to the dehumanizing influence of assembly-line production. Their suffering for their principles is presented as noble and admirable. Harry uses the walking race (a tool of the "enemy") for his own ends, turning Burton's own strength against him (a favorite Capra twist).

The walkathon nicely provides a skeleton for the picaresque story structure. The individual gag sequences, which are like climaxes from shorter Sennett comedies, are unified by the journey upon which Harry has embarked. The competition lends urgency, even when intervals of silliness prevail.

Returning periodically to the theater where Harry's father watches the progress of the race (on newsreels) also holds the narrative together, lest the viewer forget that the Elf's mission has a specific purpose. Furthermore, these recurring episodes allow Harry to clown for the newsreel cameras, adding a touch of simulated cinema verité to the proceedings.

TRAMP, TRAMP, TRAMP, with Joan Crawford (First National, 1926).   (The Museum of Modern Art, New York City)

Several gag sequences are elaborately developed.   Perhaps the best is when Harry finds himself on a chain gang. The little waif, penniless, is forced to steal some food.   The irate farmer presses charges, and very soon the Elf is "tramping" along in a chain gang (adding a double meaning to the film's title).   He looks especially wistful as he marches along in formation, his ball and chain in one hand, in the company of hardened criminals.

Soon, they have reached their destination and tools are passed out.   From an untidy pile of sledgehammers, Harry selects what looks like a tack hammer, appropriately kid-sized.   When the guard orders him to choose a bigger hammer, the heavy head slides off the handle and lands on the

guard's foot. In the ensuing confusion, Harry ends up with
the guard's rifle! The authorities quickly regain control and
shove Harry away. But the Elf has triumphed, for he holds
that little hammer firmly in one hand.

The other convicts swing high and smash large rocks.
Harry selects only the tiniest pebbles, places them on a
boulder and taps them lightly. Anything larger than a golf
ball is too big for him.

Soon he finds himself in the midst of an escape attempt. Everyone but Harry unlocks his leg irons. He
scampers toward an escaping train, his heavy iron ball in
one hand, and tosses it into a car. But now the train is
moving too fast, and Harry is forced to hop along on one
foot. A title announces: "Forty Miles Later --" ... and
Harry is still hopping along, grateful that the train is finally
stopping. While he soaks his feet in a nearby puddle (the
soles of his shoes are completely worn off), the train moves
slightly, its metal wheels shearing the chain which has draped
over one rail. Harry is free but he doesn't notice. When
the time comes for him to move on, he stoically picks up
the iron ball and chain, accepting his unnecessary burden.

Another extended routine involves Harry sharing a
room with the World Champion walker the night before the
race. The champion has already been angered by the many
pictures of Betty that Harry has torn off billboards and plas-
tered all around the room. Exasperated by the little guy,
the athlete feeds Harry several barbituates and a couple of
stiff shots of whiskey.

Edwards was not afraid to let the motionless camera
settle on a close-up of Harry and allow the star's face to
dominate the screen. The routine consisted of Harry falling
asleep. His eyes would grow hazy, and then he would suddenly jerk back to consciousness for a time. He yawns repeatedly. Instead of retiring to his bed, Harry can only curl
up on the floor with his knees pulled up, baby-style.

Obviously, much more care went into the construction
of the comedy setpieces in TRAMP, TRAMP, TRAMP than a
typical Sennett two-reeler. This almost hurts the film, for
the writers are too formalistically adhering to formula: every
gag must have several elaborations which lead to a big topper.
There is a mechanical quality to some of the action and the
believability of certain gags can be easily called into question.

The problem, as always, was not getting Langdon into trouble, but getting him out of it. Harry's intellect was fixed at an extremely low level in his first feature. He even looks smaller here than in most of his earlier shorts. He is dwarfed by his environment as he travels along the backroads. Edwards has deliberately placed Harry against taller people; even his oversized sweater reinforces the "little vs. big" theme.

How, then, could such a little pixie consistently come out on top? By providence, of course, but how would that manifest? Circumstances always had to play into his helpless hands. When Harry slides down that hill on that section of fence, the fence conveniently blocks the road for the other racers (who are just rounding the bend), even to the extent of featuring the transplanted "No Trespassing" sign for emphasis. Capra and Ripley were trying too hard to tie everything up in tidy packages.

Nor was the thorny problem of Harry's love interest adequately solved. In the shorter films, Langdon's questionable sexual prowess (and the fact that women still accepted him) could be glossed over fairly easily. In a feature, the audience expected a few more details.

Betty seems more sorry for him than in love with him. How her pity turns to love is unexplained; perhaps she marries him because he saved her life in the cyclone sequence. The transition is sudden enough that the viewer barely has time to question the chain of events; however, it was a question that would eventually have to be addressed more squarely in future films.

Harry's baby routine in the crib was at once hilarious and grotesque. Originally, they had planned to use a real baby (or so studio releases claimed). Then someone had the idea to put the 40-year-old comedian into baby clothes. The result is, for some, rather disturbing. Harry was pushing his baby character to one logical limit, further than some tastes would have preferred. The scene went over at the time, but seems somewhat excessive (though perversely fascinating) in retrospect.

With the filming completed in February 1926, TRAMP, TRAMP, TRAMP was edited to a taut 62 minutes. Laughs were clocked at previews in different cities. In every venue, the clocked laughs were long and frequent, bolstering the

confidence of Langdon and his staff.   It was set to premiere
at the Mark Strand in New York City in April.   Langdon decided to attend the premiere himself.   Frank Capra and Bill
Jenner made the trip with him.

Harry's big gamble paid off.   TRAMP, TRAMP,
TRAMP was a solid, if unspectacular, hit.   It even broke
a box-office record at Loew's State Theater in Los Angeles,
taking in $31,500 the first week.

The reviews were generally good, but a few critics
were cautious, voicing a few reservations.   Mordaunt Hall,
the rather erratic reviewer for The New York Times, wrote:
"Although Mr. Langdon undoubtedly has a keen sense of the
ridiculous, there are in this new film several episodes that
are strongly reminiscent of THE GOLD RUSH and which suffer by comparison with the Chaplin comedy."   But Hall
couldn't deny the popular reaction in his conclusion: "This
is quite a jolly entertainment and it was obviously enjoyed
by the majority of the Mark Strand audience yesterday afternoon."[5]

The majority of the critical reaction was typified by
Photoplay:

> This picture takes Harry Langdon's doleful face
> and pathetic figure out of the two-reel class and
> into the Chaplin and Lloyd screen dimensions.
> Not that he equals their standing yet, but he is a
> worthy addition to a group of comedy makers of
> which we have entirely too few.   Langdon has
> graduated and this picture is his diploma.[6]

NOTES

1.   Lax, Eric.   On Being Funny, p. 113.
2.   First National press release, April 15, 1926.
3.   "Comedy's Greatest Era," Life Magazine, September 5,
         1949, p. 80.
4.   "The Serious Side of Comedy Making," Theatre Magazine,
         December 1927, p. 22.
5.   New York Times, May 24, 1926.
6.   Photoplay, May 1926, p. 49.

Chapter Seven: A MEETING OF ANGELS

When Langdon's first feature film was completed, the Langdon Unit had its first casualty: director Harry Edwards. Most explanations for Edwards' resignation claim that TRAMP, TRAMP, TRAMP ran far over-budget, and that the director had received most of the blame. Sennett (writing twenty years later) pointed instead to Langdon himself, stating that he "blew the entire $150,000 production budget before he got his first story written."[1]

This is almost certainly an exaggeration. The Harry Langdon Corporation had agreed to deliver the first feature to First National for an April premiere. The finished product had been delivered on schedule. In fact, the entire project had taken a brief five months. In the film business, cost overruns very nearly always led to production delays, or vice versa.

Yet, Langdon himself acknowledged these money problems in an interview with Photoplay reporter Katherine Albert. Albert, recording Langdon's point of view, said that Edwards "had taken too much time on [TRAMP, TRAMP, TRAMP] and run him into the red, so Harry looked about for another director for the next one."[2]

Capra claimed that "Edwards couldn't take Langdon's present approval or disapproval of his every move."[3] Whatever the reason, the parting was amicable enough for Langdon and Edwards to remain close personal friends, and work together on future projects.

Capra finally had the opportunity to direct, which he had wanted from the moment he set foot on the Sennett lot. Edwards recommended Capra as his successor, and Langdon (who was also close to Capra) agreed to the new arrangement.

In THE STRONG MAN (September 1926), Langdon's second feature-length comedy, Harry plays a young Belgian doughboy who loves an American girl he has only known through Red Cross correspondence. [4]   The photograph she has sent gives no hint that she is blind.   To portray Mary Brown, Langdon put a young actress named Priscilla Bonner under contract.   Miss Bonner recalled in The Idols of Silence:

> I had a very small part in THE STRONG MAN. There was a very poignant scene, just where the funny-looking man stands in front of the girl to whom he is a dream man, and she can't see him, so he always will be.   She never dreamed he'd come, and she never dreamed he'd know she was blind.   It's a beautiful situation, and so they didn't want a girl who was a comedian to play it.   I think that's why I was chosen.

Gertrude Astor, a comedienne who specialized in vamp parts, was perfectly cast as Lily, the tough big-city moll. Her coarseness in the part was not only effective opposite Langdon, but enhanced the ethereal purity of Bonner's characterization.

The opening title is superimposed over a painting of a huge mountain.   The first images are those of war: explosions, gun fire, soldiers leaping from the trenches.   "No Man's Land" is the setting for Harry's first encounter with the strong man (Arthur Thalasso).

Harry seems blissfully unaware of the dangers of combat.   Instead, he is engrossed in a game of target practice. Appropriately, he is only able to knock the can of beans from the rock with a slingshot; the machine gun at his side is too adult for Harry to master.   A courier delivers a letter from Mary Brown, which includes a rather unclear photograph. Harry kisses the photo, and holds it close to his heart.

Trouble lurks in a nearby trench: Zandow, an enemy soldier (played by Thalasso), draws a bead on the elfin doughboy.   Fortunately, Harry has put his useless machine gun aside and beans the strong man with ration biscuits, again

wielding his trusty slingshot. At first, Langdon (in a pluckier
mood than usual) gamely drives the "cootie" away, but soon
finds himself taken prisoner.

After the Armistice is signed, the two former enemies
team up and take a steamer to America. Their intention is
to perform a vaudeville act: "The Great Zandow and Company." Naturally, Little Harry is the "Company," meaning
he carries the luggage. [5]

At the U. S. Immigration station on Ellis Island, Langdon performs a unique flag salute: first army style, then
his own trademark wave, certainly a more personal sign of
allegiance. He greets America with the same tentative optimism he offers any friendly stranger.

When a careless baggage handler crushes a top hat
given to the strong man by a crown prince, reducing the big
man to tears, Harry starts giving the handler a severe tongue-
lashing ... until he sees the burly size of the man. His
bravado quickly fades into a series of V-shaped smiles, winks,
and self-deprecating gestures.

Trying to escape the irate trunk-heaver, Langdon tumbles into the rear of an empty chapel, bumping the back of a
wobbly bench. It totters forward into the pew in front and
the benches start toppling like dominos. Harry, his big eyes
popping in shock, bobs up and down in panic, reaching awkward arms toward the cascading benches, helpless to stop
their progress. He runs forward, arms outstretched, always
about two feet from the crest of the wave.

Now that he has reached America, Harry is determined
to find his sweetheart. (Since they have corresponded through
the Red Cross, he doesn't know her address.) What is his
method of locating Mary? He plants himself on a bustling
New York City street corner and compares her tattered photograph to the faces of passing women!

Very soon, Langdon meets the brassy moll (Astor) who
has earlier taken note of his search. She hides a roll of hot
cash in his pocket to avoid a detective, and then (when the
cash slips into the lining of his coat) must lure him to her
apartment to recover the money. She bats her eye-lashes
demurely, introducing herself as "Little Mary. "

At first, Harry is beside himself with joy, holding her

Harry in "No Man's Land" from THE STRONG MAN (First
National, 1926).   (The Museum of Modern Art, New York
City)

hand and skipping alongside her.   But even Langdon soon
penetrates her ruse, as she lights a wicked cigarette and
brazenly hikes up her dress to reveal her legs.   When he
refuses to enter her apartment building, Lily pretends to
faint.   Reluctantly, he must carry her inside and up a long
flight of stairs.

     At one point, he deposits her limp body on the banis-
ter while trying to free his foot from a bucket.   Lily slides
down, flopping hard on the marble floor.   She is quite a load
for the little guy to carry.   Eventually, he gets the idea of
carrying her on his lap, moving backwards up the stairs in
a sitting position, one step at a time.

After Lily finally traps him in her apartment, she chases Little Harry around the room in a wild burlesque of sexual seduction. As usual with Langdon, the roles are reversed. Although she is really after the cash, Harry thinks she lusts for his body. Can he really believe her desire for him is so great that she will pull a knife on him? He does. Eventually, he lets her kiss him (giving her the chance to accomplish her real purpose) but warns her as he leaves: "Don't let this leak out. "

On the way out, Harry wanders into the art studios of a "Madame Browne" looking for Mary. He enters just in time to watch the artist's model remove her robe. Face to face with a totally naked woman, the already jittery Harry panics and tumbles down the same stairs he had struggled up just moments before.

The next sequence (after some time out for the script to make some plot points) has nothing to do with the narrative, but stands as one of Harry Langdon's best. The setting is in a bus traveling from New York to the small town of Cloverdale, where Zandow has a vaudeville engagement. It is Harry's most extended, accomplished pantomime sequence in THE STRONG MAN.

He has caught a cold. His eyes are bleary, and his nose is completely stuffed. He sneezes several times, and miserably tries to take his foul-tasting medicine. He quails several times as the spoon approaches his mouth, but finally screws up the courage. At the last moment, he sneezes the spoon's contents onto a dapper passenger seated next to him (Brooks Benedict).

Harry is apologetic, but the man's sarcastic put-downs provoke his ire. Even an Elf has his limit. His eyes narrow, and he throws a timid punch. The passenger responds with a haymaker that sends Harry reeling.

Surprisingly, the Elf doesn't drop the issue. His eyes narrow again, and his left hand forms a fist. He holds that fist for a very long time, marshalling his nerve. When he finally decides to strike, his nemesis pushes it away without even looking up from his newspaper.

All this time, the other passengers have grown increasingly irritated with the little twirp. The final straw comes when he applies (what he thinks is) a cold rub to his chest. Instead, it is fragrant Limburger cheese. "I'm beginning to smell!" Harry happily exclaims. The others

agree and throw him off the moving bus.   As the bus rapidly
traverses a tight switchback in the road, Harry rolls down
the hill and smashes through the ceiling, landing back in his
old seat.

The first half of the film represents exceptional gag
construction; the second half transcends mere gag comedy.
At last, Langdon had a chance to prove that he was not only
a brilliant comedian, but an actor of rare ability.   With the
arrival in Cloverdale, THE STRONG MAN makes its bid for
greatness.

Cloverdale has a problem: bootleggers.   The evil,
insidious forces of greed and corruption have turned the quiet
God-fearing little hamlet into a wide-open town.   The town
hall has been converted into a saloon, run by the repulsive
Mike McDevitt (Robert McKim).   The good townspeople, led
by Mary's father Parson Brown (William V. Mong), are out-
raged.   Into the middle of this conflict come Zandow and his
assistant.   Their performance has been contracted by McDevitt
for the amusement of his drunken, unruly patrons.

Backstage, Harry is looking for a place to fill a bucket with water.   A stage hand tells him: "Ask Mary Brown. "
Langdon freezes.   He turns and opens the back door, which
leads into the adjacent church yard.   There he sees Mary.

Harry goes bananas in this scene reminiscent of his
meeting with Joan Crawford in TRAMP, TRAMP, TRAMP.
He seems to run in several directions at once, as he tries
to pull himself together for his big entrance.   But as he
passes through the doorway "the jackrabbit scamper turns
into an effortless stroll, " Walter Kerr writes in The Silent
Clowns.   "I don't think even Chaplin ever shifted rhythm
more absolutely, more mysteriously. "

Harry struts his stuff before her like a feisty bantam,
a man of the world.   Still unaware that Mary is blind, he finally inquires: "Aren't you glad to see me?"   In a long-held
close-up, Mary trembles with both joy and sorrow, for here
is her dream lover, come all the way across the ocean, and
she fears she will lose him when he discovers the truth.

Wisely, Capra cuts to a few moments later, when
Harry has learned of her handicap and plainly doesn't mind.
They sit next to each other on a bench.   The moment is elec-
tric.   It is more a meeting of angels than mere mortals.

THE STRONG MAN, with Gertrude Astor (First National,
1926). (Academy Collection)

The look of boyish yearning on Harry's face is almost unbearably poignant, for one can see that he has known loneli-
ness and rejection, as Mary has.   They understand each
other, are made for each other.   It is Harry Langdon's supreme moment.   In addition to pathos, the moment effects
a deep humanity, and reveals the longing within Harry with
an honesty that is almost embarrassing.

        Quickly, lest the story bog down, Capra moves to
Harry's discovery that Zandow is drunk on bootleg whiskey
and can't perform.   But McDevitt and friends will not be
denied.   Against his will, Harry is dragged into the dressing
room.   Moments later, he emerges wearing Zandow's (over-
sized) costume.   Harry must be the strong man!

        In the costume, Langdon has finally become the jester/
fool that his character had always suggested.   With his pants
hiked high to look like dark baggy trunks, and white longjohns,

he only lacks slippers with curled toes and bells. Instead,
he wears his trusty slapshoes. Never has Harry looked more
like a pixie.

He peers meekly at the surly crowd, his knees shaking. Harry backs off, but is thrown on-stage. The crowd
cheers. Harry does a dainty curtsy or two, a kind of mild
"ta-daa" gesture, as he considers his first course of action.
He tries to lift a 400-pound weight, but can't budge the thing.

Suddenly he shows a streak of ingenuity. He rolls a
couple of iron balls into a bottomless bucket (they fall through
a hole in the stage floor) and makes a big show of lifting the
bucket. The audience applauds. He does the splits (eyes
widening as he slips down further than he'd planned); he lets
pigeons loose which had somehow hidden in his pants. He
performs a couple of silly soft-shoe dances. Langdon's
vaudeville background is being cleverly exploited here. He
seems right at home on the stage. And the audience (somewhat inexplicably) cheers his every move.

Outside, Parson Brown is leading his followers around
the saloon, singing "Onward Christian Soldiers" to bring down
the walls of Jericho. One of McDevitt's men is enraged,
shouting that they'll soon have Mary Brown performing for
their amusement.

For Harry, those are fighting words. He takes a poke
at the guy, only to get flattened. Someone picks him up and
throws him into the air. Harry lands on the trapeze (for
Zandow had planned to shoot himself out of his stage cannon
and land on the trapeze) and begins swinging over the angry
mob. A riot breaks out.

Langdon (accidentally) kicks a cork out of a barrel of
ale, dowsing the crowd. He swings toward the stage, and
pulls a huge cloth backdrop over the mob. Soon he is firing
the cannon repeatedly, until the very walls of the building
collapse, and the townspeople triumphantly drive the rabble
from their midst. Langdon later wrote,

> During the filming of THE STRONG MAN, a trick
> cannon exploded as I pulled the lanyard to fire the
> final shot of the scene. In the noise, the smoke
> and confusion, I didn't ever know there had been
> an accident. When the smoke cleared away, we
> found that one piece of the metal cannon had grazed

the back of my head, struck a musician a glancing
blow in the cheek and buried itself in the wall of
the stage. On the screen this scene was a scream. [6]

    The final scene sums up much of Harry's character.
Now the town hero, he appears in a cop uniform, swinging
a billy club. Mary wants to accompany him on his beat. At
first he refuses, but her sad look makes him change his mind.
As they walk away from the camera, Langdon trips on a
rock. Mary helps him up, dusts him off. Little Harry is
so inept that a blind woman must lead him. As they stroll
into the distance arm-in-arm, the film ends.

* * *

THE STRONG MAN was a tremendous hit. The critics pulled
out the stops:

> Harry Langdon's second laugh-provoker firmly es-
> tablishes the wistful comedian in the front ranks of
> the screen's mirth-makers. Watch out, Charlie
> and Harold!
>   It's a grand, glorious laugh from the start to
> the finish. It begins with one laugh overlapping
> the other. Chuckles are swept into howls. Howls
> creep into tears--and by that time you're ready to
> be carried out. And we don't mean maybe! [7]

    Even The New York Times found much to praise about
the film, as Mordaunt Hall reported on Sept. 7, 1926:

> Harry Langdon's latest comedy ... leaps from gag
> to gag, always giving the protagonist ample oppor-
> tunity to show his talent as a screen farceur.
> These interludes of fun, which are like short
> sketches, have precious little bearing on a coher-
> ent narrative. Nevertheless, they serve their pur-
> pose in stirring up gales of laughter.

    Hall continued: "Mr. Langdon's work in this production
displays true ability, and it is to his credit that he is more
effective in the more sober scenes than in the turbulent
streaks. " Langdon received his best reviews yet for his
touching scene with Mary Brown. Her blindness had perfectly solved the boy-girl problem. It seemed possible that
Harry could, indeed, have a successful relationship with a
woman, provided she was blind to enough of his faults.

The high level of creativity evident in most of THE
STRONG MAN does not mean that is is a perfect film.   Particularly from a contemporary point of view, the black-and-
white nature of the central conflict in Cloverdale makes it
difficult to identify with either faction.   The Bible-thumping
sanctimony of Parson Brown is barely more palatable than
the strong arm tactics of Mike McDevitt.   Yet the screenplay
clearly intends for the Parson to be admired, with the film's
title applying to him as well as Thalasso and Langdon.   Furthermore, Capra chose to ignore certain amoral aspects of
Langdon's babyish screen persona; Harry is placed firmly in
the Parson's camp, playing the first of Capra's Christian In-
nocents.   The Elf's complex dual nature would not be explored until his next film.

The violent, rip-snorting conclusion (in the accepted
formula of the Harold Lloyd comedies) may have been exciting but it distances Harry from his audience.   At the climax
of the film, the viewer gets less of Harry Langdon.   He becomes a mere pawn of the plot.   He is also required to be-
have more aggressively than usual.   He hardly needs God as
an ally.   Capra had violated his own primary concept for the
Little Elf.   (The action scenes also demanded the unfortunate
use of obvious stunt doubles.)

Still, THE STRONG MAN was a remarkable debut for
Frank Capra as a director.   Every gag was mounted simply,
cleanly, and effectively.   Harry was given room to work.   It
is Langdon's longest silent feature, running 78 minutes, yet
it is so rich in comic invention that it actually seems no
longer than TRAMP, TRAMP, TRAMP, which was 16 minutes
shorter.

In some ways, the film is a glossy compendium of (as
Capra put it) "all that Langdon could do, and do right. "[8]   Wild
slapstick is followed by lengthy monologues in close-up.   Harry falls in love and plays the hero.   He dances on stage.   He
plays a soldier, a suitor, a strong man and a cop.   His ver-
satility never found a better vehicle.   For that reason alone,
THE STRONG MAN remains Harry Langdon's greatest film,
and ranks as one of the best American comedies ever produced.   Capra deserves ample credit for creating a surefire
audience pleaser that broadened Langdon's appeal and topped
TRAMP, TRAMP, TRAMP both financially and artistically.

Langdon had more than arrived.   At the premiere of
THE STRONG MAN in New York, First National built a forty-

foot tall neon sign above the marquis depicting Harry lifting a barbell. Now he stood among the giants.

"Harry Langdon is the favorite comedian of the movie colony," Photoplay proclaimed. "Ask Harold Lloyd who gives him the biggest celluloid laugh. Ask any star. They will all say Langdon. Now he's the comic idol of Hollywood!"[9]

NOTES

1. King of Comedy, p. 142.
2. Photoplay, February 1932, p. 40.
3. The Name Above the Title, p. 66.
4. Langdon's name in the film is Paul Bergot, but for purposes of clarity, the author takes the liberty of referring to him as Harry in the following recreation of the narrative.
5. Their act was based on a real vaudeville star, Eugene Sandow.
6. Theatre Magazine, December 1927, p. 78.
7. Photoplay, November 1926.
8. Kevin Brownlow's "Hollywood" Thames Television series.
9. Photoplay, August 1926, p. 88.

Chapter Eight: "BABY DOPE FIEND"

> "I made two films with [Harry Langdon]
> but on the second picture, there was so
> much trouble. "
>   --Priscilla Bonner[1]

The success of THE STRONG MAN cemented Langdon's growing reputation as the most important new comedian of the
1920's. Although, in truth, he had little real competition
for that position (Laurel and Hardy had not yet formed their
inspired partnership), Harry had earned his accolades. From
the middle of 1924 onward, he had given a series of consistently flawless screen performances.

The natural assumption, which led most critics to pre-
dict even greater triumphs ahead, was that Langdon stood on
the threshold of a remarkable, durable career. He had (to
all appearances) vindicated himself as a producer, for the
Harry Langdon Corporation now had two certifiable hits.

But behind the scenes, the first signs of trouble were
surfacing. The Langdon Unit, surely one of the most impressive collections of comedy creators ever assembled, was beginning to show signs of strain. The comedian was feeling
increasing confidence in his ability to take a larger role in
the creative decisions.

When Harry Edwards had bowed out, Langdon had
originally been tempted to take over as director. Chaplin
directed his own films, and had gained great prestige and

admiration for his all-around command of the medium. A
silent clown who did not direct himself, it was generally
thought, was simply not as talented as one who did. [2]

But Langdon had hesitated. The time wasn't right.
He wasn't ready to plan every shot and be the leader at all
times. Even though he was the star, he often felt ill at ease
dealing with the cast and crew on the set ("I don't like people") and his grasp of the finer details of film technique was
perhaps uncertain. Performing in front of the camera had
become second nature to him. Moving behind the camera
required more confidence than Langdon had felt.

That didn't necessarily mean Langdon surrendered
creative control to Frank Capra. Harry envisioned his role
as writer/actor/producer as the primary creative force,
with his staff (director, cameraman, editor) under his em-
ploy to help him realize his ideas. Because he lacked a
certain amount of understanding of the nature of those tasks,
he may have tended to minimize their importance in deter-
mining the shape of the final product.

Capra reported that friction between himself and the
star began when the filming of THE STRONG MAN commenced
in the spring of 1926.

> Within [Langdon's] limited range ... his art ap-
> proached genius. As a director, I had two sticky
> problems. One, to keep him on the narrow beam
> of his range; the other, talking him out of scenes
> that were not in character--in front of others on
> the set--without bruising his fast-inflating ego.
> Often, he would appeal to the writers to help him
> overrule me. Surprisingly, Ripley my staunch
> collaborator, began to agree with him more and
> more. [3]

When THE STRONG MAN was completed, everyone
knew they had a hit. Harry decided to take a well-deserved
vacation. He had had few opportunities to relax since the
move to First National. Ripley and Capra remained at the
studio. Harry's third feature[4] was in the writing stages,
and was scheduled to begin filming in November. Langdon,
Capra and Ripley had worked out the basic story and most
of the gag sequences that were to become LONG PANTS, and
Harry was content to let his staff put on the final touches.

Harry with his small-town girl (Priscilla Bonner) in LONG
PANTS (First National, 1927).   (Anthony Slide Collection)

          Capra and Ripley argued.   According to Langdon, Rip-
ley wanted Harry's entrance earlier in the picture. [5]   Apparently Capra wanted to make some plot points first, building
more slowly to the star's first entrance.   They had disagreed
before, but somehow the give-and-take had evaporated from
their partnership.

          Capra later explained that the very basis of his theory
on the making of films is the "one man - one film" concept.
In essence, he felt that films shouldn't be made by committee;
that the final decisions must rest with the director and no one

else. He later proved that he had the talent to make that theory workable. But could he have full control of a film being produced by another man, when that producer had no intention of surrendering that authority?

Ripley suggested they put their individual arguments before Langdon and let him decide. When Harry returned from his golfing holiday, and heard of the stalemate, he sided with Ripley.

Capra was dismayed by the decision. He felt that he knew what was best for the Little Elf. THE STRONG MAN was released to universal praise, seemingly supporting his point of view. He had no wish to see Harry's appeal diluted by inappropriate creative decisions.

In retrospect, Capra's delineation of "the narrow beam of his range"--the Christian Innocent--limited Langdon unnecessarily. Harry was emotionally and artistically more compatible with Ripley's darker view of the comic universe, and was pushing LONG PANTS in that direction. No one could argue with Capra's commercial instincts, but his point of view did not allow Langdon room to extensively investigate black comedy and film noir.

Capra saw that desire as nothing more than an egotist's wish to imitate Chaplin. According to Capra, Langdon threw frequent tantrums, screaming: "PATHOS! I want to do more pathos!!" He wrote: "The virus of conceit--alias the fat head--hit Langdon hard."

Alternate views of Langdon at this time remain elusive, allowing Capra's uncomplimentary portrait to prevail. Still, Capra's version fits the facts well enough that one must assume that Harry (dealing with presures from several fronts) reacted badly. Even Miss Bonner, who obviously had positive feelings for Harry, said: "He, like so many highly gifted men, was perhaps not too stable. He had very bad advice. It was a very complicated situation."

Capra hoped the situation could be salvaged. A few more directing credits would help solidify his reputation in Hollywood. No such reconciliation occurred. LONG PANTS was forged in an atmosphere of rancor and ill-feeling.

In the end, Harry Langdon fired Frank Capra. Langdon and Ripley completed the editing (Capra may have assembled

a rough cut before the final break occurred) and released the
film in the early spring of 1927.

The reviews were the most enthusiastic yet. LONG
PANTS is an amazingly good film, particularly if one considers the strained conditions under which it was made. Even
though it may have ridden on the heels of the fantastic success of THE STRONG MAN, LONG PANTS is a brilliant comedy in its own right, and far different from its predecessor.
If audiences were disturbed by Langdon's bold new tangents,
an impressive showing at the box-office belies that fact.

LONG PANTS is cinematically the most interesting of
Langdon's silent features. In the opening shots, the camera
glides into the Oak Grove Public Library, focuses on the section with romantic fiction, glides past rows of books, stopping
only to show a furtive hand removing various titles. Gradually, the viewer realizes that the camera is assuming someone's point of view, and since this is a Langdon film, it is
not difficult to guess whose point of view it is.

The subjective camera technique continues as the camera glides into a house, up a ladder and through a trapdoor
into an attic room. Even though these camera movements
delay Langdon's first appearance, they subtly promote identi-
fication with him, and convey a sense of solitary, secret purpose.

Harry is first seen sitting on his bed, reading Don
Juan. He fantasizes himself as a great lover of beautiful
women. Langdon, clad in a military dress uniform climbs
up a trellis to a balcony to woo a fair damsel in the moon-
light. (This sequence was originally shown in color. [6]) The
sound of feminine laughter outside his window rouses Harry
from his daydreams. The girls giggle derisively when he
appears in his window, calling him "little boy"--all because
he is still wearing short pants.

Harry hates his short pants. He has grown into young
adulthood, but his repressive mother has refused to permit
him to graduate to long pants; she fears he will end up in
trouble if he is allowed to move into the adult world. Finally,

[Opposite:] Harry tries to impress a big city vamp (Alma
Bennett) in LONG PANTS (First National, 1927). (The Museum of Modern Art, New York City)

his father insists that she is wrong, and Harry is given his
first pair of full-length trousers.

Very soon, Harry has an opportunity to show off his
long pants. Big-city vamp (and heroin smuggler) Bebe Blair
(Alma Bennett) stops her expensive chauffeur-driven conver-
tible in front of Harry's house, while a flat tire is replaced.
Harry is totally captivated by her worldly allure and smol-
dering sexuality. In one of the funniest scenes in LONG
PANTS, Little Harry naively tries to impress world-weary
Bebe by displaying his bicycle-riding prowess. He circles
around and around her car (there is one masterful overhead
shot), performing acrobatic stunts. Eventually, she even
allows Harry to kiss her, although her face reveals no emo-
tion.

When Harry is called away to the telephone, Bebe's
cynicism is made clear: "Let's get out of here before that
boob comes back," she instructs her chauffeur. Inside his
house, Harry's nominal girlfriend, Priscilla (Priscilla Bonner) is on the telephone, inviting him to something called
the Egg Festival. He quickly ends the conversation to get
back to Bebe. He is crestfallen to find her gone, until he
discovers a note (not meant for him) she has accidentally
dropped. Addressed "dearest one," signed "always," it
promises marriage. Harry dances ecstatically in front of his
house. Bursting with pride, he warns his parents: "Don't
be surprised if I get married soon." Harry has hopelessly
fallen in love.

Time passes. When Bebe never returns, Harry reluctantly agrees to marry Priscilla. But he can't get Bebe
out of his mind. On his wedding day, he reads in the newspaper that she has been arrested in the city (falsely, he is
certain) and assumes that that is why she never returned.
He abandoned her, and now he has to save her. But how
can he go off to the city when he is marrying Priscilla?

There is only one way out. He must get rid of Priscilla. All he can think of is Bebe; nothing else, not even a
human life, is as important. The logic of its necessity is
sufficient for Harry to carry out the murder. Quivering with
fear, he grabs an old pistol and leads unsuspecting Priscilla
(in her wedding dress) to the nearby woods. Soon she is
closing her eyes and counting to 500 in a game of hide-and-
seek.

In The Crazy Mirror, Raymond Durgnat wrote that
Langdon

> acts out the impulses which only cross our minds,
> and of course accident, i. e. fate, plays ... the
> role of our moral repressions.
>
> But of all American innocents, funny or serious,
> in any art form, only Langdon comes so near an
> adult's recreation of that absolute state of baby
> greed, baby gloating and baby blandness in selfish-
> ness. The Surrealists are quite right to claim him
> for their own, for there's never any real reason
> why he shouldn't, if it suited him, perpetrate the
> archetypal surrealist act: taking a revolver and
> firing at random into the street.

When James Agee nicknamed Langdon the "baby dope
fiend," he was referring to the contradictory impulses displayed by the comedian in LONG PANTS. Not that Little
Harry actually took dope. (He did briefly smoke an opium
pipe innocently enough in FEET OF MUD.) Agee's nickname
was an attempt to describe the nightmarish quality that Langdon unleashed in this, and subsequent films. For the word
"dope" not only fit Harry's simple-minded imbecility, but it
describes the hallucinatory quality that makes Langdon's last
silent films explorations of the darker regions of the unconscious mind.

Naturally, Harry's attempts to shoot Priscilla fail at
every turn. First, he can't get the over-sized gun out of
his tuxedo pocket. Then he drops the pistol among a pile of
dead leaves and has great difficulty recovering it. A low-
hanging tree branch pushes his top hat down over his face,
and he stumbles into a barbed wire fence. When he frees
himself from the barbed wire, he steps into an animal trap.
The trap is tied to a sapling. Every time Harry tries to
run away, the tree bends and smashes him to the ground.
Priscilla finishes counting, and opens her eyes to see her
fiancé's savage punishment.

Even the lighter moments have a dark side. Once
Harry reaches the city, he performs another remarkable
comic monologue when he finds (what he thinks is) a cop sitting on top of a crate that Bebe is hiding inside. From
across the street, Langdon can't tell that the "cop" is actually a lifelike mannequin placed there by a nearby theatrical
company. Harry knows that the police are looking for the
escaped Bebe Blair. He must lure the cop away.

He waves but gets no response.   He pretends he is
being held up by an unseen assailant.   Finally, he feigns a
heart attack on the sidewalk.   One feels that the Elf would
even die for Bebe, so one-pointed is his devotion.   Even his
feigned death struggle fails to move the cop.   Instead, a
store owner spots Harry's plight and tosses a bucket of water
on him.   Then someone picks up the dummy, and Harry realizes his mistake.   Angrily, he flings a brick at another
"dummy"--which turns out to be a flesh-and-blood policeman,
much to Harry's surprise.

The climactic scene is brutally realistic and seamy
like a cheap pulp novel.   Bebe and Harry surreptitiously
enter the backstage dressing room of her rival, a dance hall
girl who works in a cabaret.   Harry watches with mounting
dismay as Bebe corners the girl and nearly tears her limb
from limb.   When her jilted ex-lover appears on the scene,
they shoot each other to death, with Harry tremulously watching.   The cops storm into the room, and Harry (his right
arm in a sling) ends up in jail.

Harry's return to Oak Grove, his family, and fiancée
is accomplished in a series of short shots, each dissolving
into the next.   The camera dollies ahead of Harry.   He is
still in shock, hardly able to think.

When Harry returns to his house, he slips into his
usual seat at the dinner table unnoticed, and joins his family
in silent prayer.   The prayer over, he catches his mother's
eye, smiling as if to say "I'm back!"   But is everything back
to normal?

In previous films, Harry's clean mental slate might
be temporarily soiled, but the experience was forgotten at
the conclusion.   Harry rarely if ever benefited from experi-
ences, and adversities didn't dent his optimistic world view.
But for the first time, the story was constructed to center
on the lesson he had learned.   LONG PANTS is about the
rites of passage to manhood.   Harry seems to be on his way.

Yet Ripley's viewpoint cast that journey from innocence
to experience as something analogous to the passage from optimism to melancholy.   In a more realistic universe, one that
recognized the potency of evil, Little Harry was too pathetic
to consistently triumph.   For in the end of LONG PANTS,
Harry's romantic dreams are shattered.   His family's em-

brace can only satisfy for a short time; small town banality
and repression had driven him away to begin with.   What is
left for him?   Langdon and Ripley weren't ready to supply
an answer.   That would have to wait until Harry's next feature.

NOTES

1. Slide, Anthony.   The Idols of Silence.
2. Although they did not receive screen credit, both Harold
    Lloyd and Buster Keaton either directed or co-directed
    most of their best silent films.
3. The Name Above the Title, pp. 67, 68.
4. Langdon did appear in one scene in another feature:
    Colleen Moore's ELLA CINDERS (1926), for First
    National.
5. Photoplay, February 1932, p. 40.
6. Some thirty films between 1925 and 1930 featured color
    sequences.   Although full three-color Technicolor
    wasn't introduced until the middle 1930's, hand-colored
    motion pictures had existed as early as 1895.

Chapter Nine: TIME CAPSULE

The film-by-film development of Harry's comic character and universe was disrupted by Mack Sennett. When Langdon had reached his peak in popularity in the spring of 1927 (nearly eighteen months after they had severed their professional association), Sennett released a feature film starring the comedian that had collected dust in his vault since 1925. HIS FIRST FLAME (1927) was, for all intents and purposes, a brand new Langdon film.

Sennett's ploy would not be the first or last time a producer released an older film that featured an actor who had subsequently gone on to greater fame. In contemporary times, the list is substantial: Bo Derek, Robin Williams, Brooke Shields, Bette Midler, Sylvester Stallone. In earlier times, B-film outfits often re-released films when a newcomer got lucky and gained mass popularity. Virtually all actors who passed from Poverty Row to the prestigious studios found that their pasts came back to haunt them.

Langdon's situation had two basic differences from the usual pattern. First, HIS FIRST FLAME was not a re-release. It had been deliberately withheld from the theaters. Due to financial pressures, very few completed pictures have been held back from release for more than a few months. In nearly every case, the product was shipped to the exhibitors posthaste.

Second, the comedian could not have been embarrassed by the contents of the unexpected time capsule. Most often, the material from an actor's early career hardly merits a

revival. The gimmick with the most recent examples frequently involves a well-known personality either partially or
totally nude. Some of the victimized stars have resorted to
legal recourse to stop the exploitation of their careers, charg-
ing that the older films do not fairly represent their current
standards.

Langdon had no cause to be ashamed of the Sennett
film, for HIS FIRST FLAME ranks with SATURDAY AFTER-
NOON and FIDDLESTICKS as one of the best of the comedies
shot in Edendale. In addition, Langdon probably received his
share of the profits (which in 1927 would have been considerable). Although later events may have been adversely affected by its delayed release, it was initially another feather
in the comedian's cap.

Although it is difficult to discover the various circumstances that led to the shelving of HIS FIRST FLAME in 1925,
Sennett's motives cannot be difficult to surmise. About the
time the Old Man announced that he would star his newest
comedian in a full-length feature, he became aware that he
would soon lose Langdon, as he had lost all his other major
stars. His contacts certainly informed him that Harry was
considering offers from other studios. He could try to match
their financial offers, but could never offer Langdon the creative autonomy that Harry wanted so badly. Sennett concocted
a plan to cash in on Langdon's probable success elsewhere.
After Hornbeck had completed the editing, Sennett withdrew
HIS FIRST FLAME from his release schedule, and patiently
sat on it for two years.

Sennett was not without Harry Langdon films to feed
the public's appetite. While Harry was releasing TRAMP,
TRAMP, TRAMP and THE STRONG MAN for his own corporation, Mack Sennett was constantly re-issuing the comic's
older films. For a time, his Langdon catalog was a gold
mine. Still, they could only make the rounds so many times
before they became overexposed--probably some time in early
1927. And so, Sennett released HIS FIRST FLAME a few
weeks after LONG PANTS debuted (thus benefiting from First
National's expensive publicity campaign for the "official"
Langdon film). Harry's career was at its zenith. He had
two new feature films in simultaneous release!

The opening title of HIS FIRST FLAME read, "They
say 'Love is the only fire against which there is no insurance.' " By implication, romantic impulses are fraught with

HIS FIRST FLAME, with Ruth Hiatt (Sennett/Pathe, 1927).
(The Museum of Modern Art, New York City)

danger.   The first scene quickly establishes that Ethel (Natalie Kingston), Harry's first flame, is a golddigger who considers sincere love old-fashioned.   Her younger sister, Mary
(Ruth Hiatt), listens to her sister's frank expressions of
greed, and mildly retorts: "I'd love Harry even if he didn't
have a cent. "   The bad sister/good sister dichotomy is set.

Harry reveals his naivete and starry-eyed adoration
of the "fairer" sex when he addresses an all-female audience
(he has just graduated from college) on the subject: "Women
--and why. "   This is a fitting title for a Langdon film, for
its vagueness (like Harry's own) nevertheless communicates
much.   He is aware of those who fail to appreciate the virtues and contributions of women to society, and he passionately defends them to his very receptive audience.

Harry Howells assumes an exhortive oratory technique,
with big gestures and a series of inappropriate platitudes about
women such as, "What this country needs is more matrimony

and less alimony!" and "Half my ancestors were women!!"
(Title composer A. H. Giebler wrote amusing "dialogue" only
occasionally. Perhaps with lesser talents, these joke titles
could contribute a few laughs, but Langdon's style of humor
somehow seemed above such obvious laugh-begging. The
titles are the consistent flaw that runs through both the Sennett films and even the best of the independent features, although the features are generally better in this respect.)

The crowd responds enthusiastically (and improbably)
to everything Harry says, even rushing the stage to congratulate him. The ocean of women that surge toward him scares
the hell out of Harry. He is clearly a young man who puts
his women on pedestals; dealing with them in real life (re-
conciling fantasy versus fact) proved difficult for him.

No one espouses the opposite view of women more
than Harry's fireman uncle, Amos McCarthy (Vernon Dent).
Too many singed love affairs have left him an embittered
misogynist. In his capacity as Harry's relative and nominal
guardian, Amos is determined to keep his dim-witted nephew
from falling under their influence.

When Harry arrives at the firehouse, he announces
that his first intention after graduating is to marry his sweetheart and settle down to a life of wedded bliss. Langdon contributes his finest pantomimic routine in HIS FIRST FLAME
as he slowly realized that his words are not meeting with his
uncle's favor. Amos grimaces, his eyes bulging. Harry im-
mediately retreats, avowing to think it over. He even gives
the flowers and candy intended for Ethel to his Uncle.

Moments after leaving the fire station, and having pur-
chased another bouquet and box of candy, Howells loses the
wedding ring when his old school friend Hector (Bud Jamison)
pats him heartily on the back and the gold band apparently
rolls into the street.

While the prospective groom chases nonsensically
around the city sidewalks in a frantic search, Amos decides
to take action. He telephones Ethel and informs her that
Harry is completely broke. Ethel stomps on her wedding
gown and throws his photograph into the fire. Little Mary
carefully folds the gown and puts it into its box.

Harry discovers Ethel's change of heart when he follows his uncle to the site of a blazing apartment fire. Not

HIS FIRST FLAME, with Vernon Dent (Sennett/Pathe, 1927).
(The Museum of Modern Art, New York City)

officially on the force (and clad in ridiculously large fireman's pants), Howells is at first content to sit on the opposite curb and proudly point out that the man climbing the tall
ladder is his uncle.   When a woman leaps from the burning
building to a safety net, Harry applauds mildly.   The specta-
cle is just a show to him until he recognizes his fiancée in
one of the windows, screaming for help.   Harry is on his
feet at once, and after one or two rebuffs, plunges into the
smoke-filled building.

However, Amos reaches Ethel first.   After recovering
from the effects of the smoke, Ethel wastes little time making a play for McCarthy.   Harry appears just in time to
watch them climb into a cab together.   (Amos will apparently

have to learn his own lesson again.) The Elf watches forlornly as they kiss. The sight of his sweetheart in his uncle's arms leaves him stunned.

Having watched Harry's humiliation, and recognizing
her chance, Mary decides to stage her own rescue. After
lighting a tiny fire in a vase, she telephone for help. Harry
is alone at the firehouse. The others have gone out on another call, leaving him to mind the store. He stands de-
jectedly facing away from the camera. At his feet, tear
drops fall onto the dusty floor.

The call to action does not initially rouse Harry.
"I'll tell the boys about it when they get back," he replies
distractedly. Eventually, Mary manages to convince Harry
to come on his own. He fires up the old-fashioned steam
engine (adding an old stuffed mattress to the fire, along with
some coal), hitches up the horses, dons a fireman's hat,
and rides to the rescue.

The horses run out of control around Mary's house
several times until Howells brings them to a stop. The engine is positioned near the house, with the bellowing smoke
(that mattress) wafting into an upper window. Soon, Mary
fears that she is in serious danger, while Harry ineffectually
(and quite nimbly) stumbles about outside.

First, he knocks on the front door and waits patiently
for an answer. When the firehose loses pressure, he throws
a few feeble handfuls of water toward the house. Finally inside, he lights a match to see his way through the spreading
smoke. After tossing the spent match away, Harry thought-
fully returns to fastidiously snuff out the smoking match with
his foot. Yards away, the house is (seemingly) inundated in
flames.

Back outside, the neophyte firefighter hoists a ladder
to an upper balcony and the escape is accomplished. Harry
carries Mary in his arms. Suddenly Amos McCarthy runs
up to assess the situation. Face-to-face with the one who
had "stolen" his first flame, Harry warily backs away a few
steps. Pulling the girl tighter to him, he turns and carries
her down the street, away from danger.

*   *   *

Superficially, HIS FIRST FLAME is little more than an ex-
ceptionally well-written and acted boy-meets-girl story. Yet

the gags themselves rarely stop at ordinary slapstick. They have at their core some comment (often ironic) on the old-fashioned values (love, marriage, children) that Harry Howells espouses.

Like the world of 1920's audiences, Harry's world (in most of his silent films, including this one) is poised on the brink of changing values and social concepts. Often these traditional values seemed linked to small town life. The increasingly complex, fast-paced city life unfailingly presented him with a series of disillusioning, even shocking situations. Capra and Ripley ended their collaboration with the most explicit treatment of this subject in LONG PANTS.

Harry Howells makes several wrong assumptions about the proper course of true love. When he follows a young couple who push a baby carriage, he enviously predicts: "I'll soon be pushing a baby buggy myself." The bundle of joy is really stolen merchandise, for the "young couple" are actually shoplifters using the carriage as a cover. Marriage can lead to children, yes; it can also lead to theft.

One of the comic sequences that only generally relates to the emerging man-woman theme also provides Harry with a showcase for a routine that he repeated often in other films. In the course of his many travails, Harry was often mistaking dummies for real people. [1] In HIS FIRST FLAME, the opportunity came when Harry tried to rescue Ethel in the apartment fire. The next the viewer sees of Harry, he is climbing out a high window onto a ladder. The seat of his pants emits a thick cloud of smoke; he carries a wooden dummy with one arm (as he would a real person).

For a very long time, Langdon does not penetrate the reality of the situation. Even after suspecting the truth, he continues talking to "her"--just in case. Finally, a close examination reveals the rather obvious fact that the mannequin's eyes are painted on its face. Abruptly an object of such worth becomes worthless garbage, at once discarded.

In HIS FIRST FLAME, Harry dressed as a woman, although not voluntarily. The lady shoplifter steals his own clothes for a disguise, leaving Harry clad in her dress and hat. Still woozy from the attack (and being forcibly stripped), he tries to summon taxi after taxi. Finally, a car stops and Harry climbs in. Moments later, the car screeches to a halt, depositing Harry on the street. He looks terrified!

That whatever occurred in the car remained unseen provides
an ambiguous buffer that adds to the comedy. Obviously,
the passenger made a pass at him. Harry's pale countenance
conveys that much. But does the passenger need glasses?
Can he have really mistaken Howells for a female? If not,
the Elf has just been propositioned by his first homosexual!

The recognition of the threatening nature of the real
world ties HIS FIRST FLAME with the other silent feature
films, especially LONG PANTS. The Sennett film is not as
single-minded in its examination of the effects of a cold,
cruel world on the Elf's psyche. Any effort the writers made
toward developing a coherent theme was diffused by the ten-
dency toward fast gag comedy. No definitive statement on
womankind emerged.

Nor does the Sennett feature have production values
that match the First National series. The budget seems
well within the normal range for Langdon short comedies of
this period. There are no lavish sets or involved location
shots. The most expensive scene is the apartment fire,
which was certainly filmed on a standing set on the Sennett
lot. The extras could not have cost much. It probably cost
no more than $75,000 to produce--about half of the budget
for an independent feature.

In a sense, Harry scooped Mack Sennett on one major
point, for he had also played his own child in HIS FIRST
FLAME which was unreleased when TRAMP, TRAMP, TRAMP
adapted the routine for its conclusion. The New York Times
wrote:

> Possibly the best effect of all in this current ven-
> ture ... is where the wistful Harry gazes into a
> shop window and visualizes his own offspring, im-
> personated by himself. The eyes are, of course,
> those of the father, and so is the queer little mouth.
> Mr. Langdon is at his best in this humorous piece
> of work. [2]

This scene has inexplicably been cut from the prints currently
available for rental.

What HIS FIRST FLAME lacks in cinematic style and
narrative development, it compensates with its upbeat mood
and plentiful gags. If it looked lightweight in comparison
with LONG PANTS, it provided a pleasant change of pace before the release of Langdon's most controversial silent film.

NOTES

1. Other films with dummy routines: LONG PANTS,
   SOLDIER MAN, FEET OF MUD, COUNSEL ON DE
   FENCE, KNIGHT DUTY, and MISBEHAVING HUS-
   BANDS.
2. The New York Times, May 7, 1927.

Chapter Ten: SAD CLOWN

The opening image of THREE'S A CROWD (1927) is one of
the most enchanting of silent cinema. The viewer looks down
a city street from a raised perspective. It is dawn. Early
risers sleepily emerge from their darkened rooms to carry
on their lives. A milkman makes his early morning rounds.
The streetlights blink off as sunlight suffuses the sidewalks
and alleys.

The camera moves in closer and peers down a particularly wide alley to reveal a distinctly peculiar sight: a
shack, box-like, suspended crazily fifty feet up the side of
one wall. It is mounted on supports that look far too fragile.
A stove pipe juts upward from the angled roof.

The access is equally strange: one long stairway,
fifty continuous steps, straight up. Like the shack, the stairway is stuck impossibly against the brick wall, as if by glue.
Both structures evoke a bizarre, hallucinatory atmosphere.

Inside the shack, an alarm clock signals the hour of
5 a.m. and the Little Elf is first seen as he groggily reaches
out a hand to shut off the racket. He sits up woozily. He
is wearing a flannel nightgown and cap. He yawns, feebly
trying to clear away the mists of sleep. He blinks, unseeing.
Moments later, he is snoring again.

A second alarm comes in the form of the loud bullhorn
voice of his furious boss, which finally penetrates even Harry's
deep sleep. He stumbles to the window, blearily peering down
at the burly figure of his boss, who shakes his fist and further exhorts the Elf to get moving.

Still in a daze, Harry methodically prepares for his day. The inside of his one-room abode is modest but orderly. It contains a bed in the center, a streetlight rigged as an indoor lamp, shelves with a few meager provisions, a stove and a few grimy windows. His shower is a makeshift affair: a suspended watering can, a washtub and a rigged curtain. In goes Harry (modestly removing his nightgown after entering) and down tips the watering can.

Harry's boss has grown angrier. He picks up a rock, throws it toward the cabin. His aim is high, and the rock knocks the stovepipe off the roof. Inside, the pipe--loose now--swings in a quick arc and dumps its sooty contents directly into the shower.

Poor Harry! He comes to the window, covered totally with viscous black tar, looking like nothing so much as a character from Uncle Remus. Any soot that has escaped the moisture of the shower has gone to his nose. He sneezes repeatedly, causing his flabby ebony cheeks to vibrate. Only his hair belies the tar baby impersonation. Its fuzziness remains, though it is thickly coated with coal dust.

Several hours later, Harry is (at last) ready to report for work. He takes a final, fastidious whisk broom to his coat. He's wearing his standard tight coat with the eight big buttons, and his felt hat with the hatbrim turned up all around. Just as he scampers down the long stairway, a lunch whistle blows.

His long-suffering employer watches as Harry contentedly settles down and opens his lunch pail. He removes its sole contents: a cup and saucer, already filled to the brim with hot coffee. The coffee is just one more impossible fait accompli, like Harry's stairway, his shack, and his own existence.

Harry longingly watches his boss (who also lives off the same alley, in nicer quarters) play with his young son. Harry looks depressed. An awareness of his bleak lifestyle is quickly communicated. He is a lowly moving man who works twelve hours a day for a pittance, only to return home to his lonely room to catch a few hours sleep before reporting for work again. Harry now had a job that formalized his perpetual burdens.

The Elf's eye catches something interesting in the

trash. It is an old cloth doll that someone has cast aside.
It bears an unmistakable resemblance to Little Harry, particularly in its facial blankness.

His boss notices the resemblance right away, laughing
uproariously at the joke. Harry is not so sure of the humor
of the comparison. He plays gingerly with the doll, all the
while watching his boss play with his flesh-and-blood offspring.
He tries to make it stand on his hand; the doll collapses limply
to the alley floor. It is clearly no substitute for the real
thing.

The employer's wife beckons Harry. "There's a wife
and child for every good man," she reassures him soothingly.
Harry listens stoically, not daring to allow himself to react.
He seems emotionally numb. When lunch is over, his boss
tosses the doll back into the garbage.

A montage sequence shows the passing of the seasons.
Winter comes to the city, attacking with a vengeance. A
blinding snow storm causes one after another pedestrian to
conk their heads on a single street sign. The camera picks
out one figure, a woman, as she weaves in the onslaught of
the blizzard. Seeking to avoid the wind, she turns into Harry's alley, and collapses onto the packed snow at the base
of his stairway.

By the time he finds her, she is unconscious. Hesi-
tantly, he approaches her. He backs off a few steps, looking
around for help. There is no one. Harry gently picks her
up and carries her up to his cabin. Soon she is laying on
his bed, and he is trying to make her more comfortable. He
rubs her hands, undoes her scarf and ragged coat.

In the process of his ministrations, Harry uncovers
something odd: tiny clothes, small knitted booties. He
blinks slowly. Comprehension dawns. Excitement fills him,
and he seems to take leave of his senses as he runs around
his tiny room.

Harry's shack is the scene of the miracle of birth.
Harry wanted to watch, but the neighborhood midwives and
local doctors (for Harry had gamely corralled three or four
reluctant physicians) repeatedly kick him outside. Wistfully,
Harry waits on the landing, leaving his vigil only long enough
to buy some toys for the child: a drum, a toy rifle, a pair
of skates.

Harry and "friend" in THREE'S A CROWD (First National,
1927).   (The Museum of Modern Art, New York City)

Eventually, the crowd leaves. They congratulate him on their way out, assuming he is the father. Harry tentatively enters the room, stopping several feet from the bed. Mother and child are doing fine. Harry seems to be rooted to the spot. He stares and stares. The Elf is still standing transfixed as the scene slowly fades to black.

At last, Harry has a family all his own. His good fortune leaves him in a daze. He can't take his eyes off the girl (Gladys McConnell). He is so entranced that he scarcely can pay any attention to his own actions. When he pulls a frozen diaper off the clothes line, he tries to soften it by using a rolling pin on it. As he stares adoringly at her, he automatically covers it with flour, trims it over a pie tin, and fills it with fruit. Only when he has completed his diaper pie, and holds it in one hand, does it gradually (very gradually) dawn on him what he has done.

Even inexperienced Harry knows that where there is a mother and child, there is also (somewhere) a father. He finds a picture of the husband among her things and surreptitiously takes it aside. His eyes narrow; holding the photo in one hand, he punches it delicately two or three times. Then he cautiously slips it back on the bedside table.

Unable to shake feelings of foreboding, the Elf consults a fortune-teller. After reading Harry's palm, the Swami assures Harry that everything will work out in his favor. He has nothing to worry about. Harry steals questioning glances at his palm, trying to see what the Swami sees.

At home, the still-weak mother gives Harry her crying infant to hold. Having fashioned a makeshift rocking cradle big enough for both the baby and himself, Harry climbs in. He begins rocking, moving like the pointer of a metronome; faced straight ahead, his head traces and retraces a series of perfect arcs.

In a single long-held camera take, Harry performs tricks to stop the baby's bawling. When he crosses his eyes, he becomes extremely befuddled when one eye at first refuses to uncross. He puffs his already puffy cheeks full of air, looking like a demented chipmunk. The continuous rocking motion has its desired effect on both babes. Soon they are asleep, and the movement of the cradle stops. All is calm.

Suddenly the room darkens. Stormy weather outside brings a wind that whips the curtains and sends the street-light by the bed swinging wildly. Eerie lights flash outside, illuminating the room with an otherworldly glow.

Harry is awakened by the storm to a different reality. Now he inhabits the netherworld of his dreams--or, more ac-curately, his nightmares. Quivering and wide-eyed, the Elf turns to the window and sees the contorted, evil face of his rival, lit by flickering lightning, leering menacingly into the room.

Abruptly, Harry's shack dissolves into a surrealistic boxing ring, lit by glazing lights and surrounded by total darkness. In one corner stands meek Little Harry. In the other is his rival, easily twice Harry's size. Their audience consists solely of the girl. She smiles up at Harry encour-agingly, instructing him how to punch.

This fires up Harry. He throws a few scrappy punches into the air, and strikes several "fearsome" boxing poses. As the husband closes in, however, Harry discovers that his boxing gloves have mysteriously grown to enormous proportions. He can barely move them. His opponent, find-ing Harry helpless, lands one punch after another.

The girl switches her allegiance. She begins rooting instead for her husband. Her eyes glaze over, and she takes to biting and tearing at her hat with her teeth. Harry's fight for his fair damsel (now a wicked witch) is doomed, and he is soon out for the count.

Harry awakens from his nightmare in time to see the repentant father enter his shack. He and the girl have a tearful reunion, leaving Harry standing off to one side, help-lessly watching. His manner radiates resignation and wistful sadness. He knows that his unspoken love for the mother and child will not be enough to hold them.

The husband thanks Harry for his help and generosity. Harry manages a weak smile, not knowing how to act in the face of such a crushing blow. "Maybe we'll see you again some time," they say. He wraps his wife in his expensive overcoat (the quality of which Harry duly notes). Having said their obligatory words of thanks, the couple quickly exits.

Harry stands in the open doorway, watching them de-

scend the stairs. Snow is gently falling. Harry carries a
lamp down to the snow-covered street, trying to see where
they have gone. Realizing it is nearly dawn, he blows out
the lamp. At that precise moment, all the streetlights blink
off, almost in sympathy. Startled, Harry runs up the stairs
for the refuge of his room.

 Epilog: The next day, Harry returns to the storefront
of the Swami fortune-teller. He glares balefully at the estab-
lishment, then at his palm. He picks up a brick, almost
throws it. He hesitates. He looks back at his misread palm,
trying to fire up his thoughts of revenge.

 He can't do it. What's the use? He turns, and tosses
the brick away. It snaps the fragile brace that restrained a
huge metal drum, maybe six feet in diameter, and the drum
crashes into the storefront like a steamroller, totally demol-
ishing it. Harry's hands fly to his hat brim, his eyes pop
in shock, and he wavers indecisively for only a short moment before he runs. End of film.

* * *

Harry Langdon was on his own now. THREE'S A CROWD is
a far more idiosyncratic, personal work than his first three
Capraesque feature films. Although Capra told Walter Kerr
that the scenario could have been started before Langdon fired
him, the sensibilities in the finished film are clearly antithe-
tical to Capra's concept of the Elf.

 Langdon liked to expound on the tragic underpinnings
of comedy: "Most deliciously comic moments on the outside,
are full of sad significance for those who realize the sinister
characterization of the situation."[1] Similar theories had been
bubbling close to the surface in Langdon's mind for years.
In an interview conducted upon the release of TRAMP, TRAMP,
TRAMP, Harry had described some guidelines for the Elf:
"I must be wretched, and consequently ludicrous. When I
do a part in a film, I must really suffer. In my pictures I
allow myself to be a victim of Fate. But a sort of Divine
providence always carries me through."[2] A year later, the
forces of chaos had gained ground. In THREE'S A CROWD,
God has deserted the Elf.

 Harry's otherworldly innocence leads not to salvation
but to damnation. In Jean-Paul Sartre's No Exit, three people who hate each other are trapped together in a room for

THREE'S A CROWD (First National, 1927).   (The Museum
of Modern Art, New York City)

all eternity. Harry's enforced isolation seems no less hor-
rifying a postulation of Hell.

The film's depiction of a malevolent universe is a remarkable cinematic achievement. THREE'S A CROWD may
be the grimmest of all fairy tales ever produced by a major
American comedian. One appreciates the regions that Langdon was exploring for their audacity and originality. Raymond Durgnat wrote: "Harry Langdon gropes, from some
virginal limbo, over the threshold of our mad, half real
world, opening up weird spaces and emptiness all around
himself, and within us."[3]

His shack could not exist on street level, with a quick
entry into the mainstream of bustling city life. Instead,
Harry is tucked in a most unlikely corner of the cityscape
and held at arm's length by the single, long stairway. His
cabin hangs on the brick wall like an insect before the mag-
nifying glass of the cinematic rectangle. As the viewer
watches Harry move about in his preparations for his work
day, it is almost with clinical interest. Harry has even dis-
tanced himself from his audience.

Cameraman Elgin Lessley must be credited with the
solid, claustrophobic look of the alley walls. The cold bricks,
the impersonal windows, all seem to surround Harry, offering hard contrast to the psychological mush of his hazy con-
sciousness. Yet he is aware of those walls, with the in-
grained awareness that a prisoner has of his cell walls and
bars. Harry's emotional paralysis, best illustrated in his
conversation with his employer's wife ("There's a wife and
child for every good man.") attests to that awareness. A
generous impulse on her part cannot help. An Elf cannot
fit in with real human beings, and Harry knows it. He is,
however, stuck in a human body; some part of him yearns
for the things that others around him have.

Harry announced to the trade press before filming began that his first self-directed feature would be more than
just a series of gags strung together. Mordaunt Hall had
written of LONG PANTS: "Mr. Langdon has once again ca-
pitulated to his omnipotent band of gag men. It may be all
very well for Harold Lloyd to rely on mechanical twists, but
Langdon possesses a cherubic countenance which offers him
a chance in other directions."[4] Langdon agreed. He felt he
had potential to be more than a mere gagster. He was not
alone in that opinion. Thirty years later, Stan Laurel called

him "a great comedian who had it in him to be a great actor, like Chaplin."[5]

Not that he hadn't achieved depth and profundity in his previous performances. His tender love scene with the blind Mary Brown would be difficult to improve upon. It is near perfect. But the exigencies of fast-paced gag comedy and mechanical plot devices quickly pulled Harry from his girl's side, breaking the spell.

What might the two new lovers have done next? Where might they have spent their first evening together? How would their courtship proceed? The viewer is deprived of sharing in the Elf's most successful relationship with a woman. Instead, Mary is relegated to the background until the denouement.

In order to develop his character further, Langdon needed to create a narrative with a fuller sense of environment, richer atmosphere and stronger, more challenging statements of theme. Like many great comedy talents, from Charlie Chaplin to Woody Allen, Langdon--at the peak of his popularity--chose to tinker with the formula that had originally brought him recognition. He wanted to be funny, and he also wanted to be taken seriously. A major ad for THREE'S A CROWD announced in bold letters: "It's Funny--and It's Art!"

THREE'S A CROWD has greater narrative cohesion than any of Langdon's silent features. Although by no means without peripheral gags, the screenplay (written by Langdon, Ripley, Robert Eddy and James Langdon, Harry's brother) stresses unity of time, place, and action. By the conclusion, the viewer is reacting to the cumulative effect of the story, rather than leaving the theater remembering individual comedy bits. The story works as a whole.

Of the framing gag (the streetlights that blink off at dawn) Walter Kerr wrote:

> That is a most striking kind of architecture--not narrative architecture precisely but gag architecture

[Opposite:] THREE'S A CROWD, with Helen Hayward and Gladys McConnell (First National, 1927). (The Museum of Modern Art, New York City)

so patiently planned and so extensive in scope that
it holds the entire narrative firmly in place between the "plant" and the "payoff" of a single gentle jest.   A joke wraps the film in its arms. [6]

The nightmare sequence depicts the central conflict
with notable economy.   Harry had earlier punched his rival's
photograph; it is only appropriate that he have his chance to
square off in a boxing ring with the actual person.   The mas-
terstroke is that the confrontation takes place in a dream,
for Langdon's subconscious mind is the source of much of
his unaccountable behavior.

Over the years, the most often repeated analysis of
THREE'S A CROWD has been that it is an out-and-out imitation of Chaplin's THE KID (1921).   Certain elements of the
story are undeniably similar.   Both comics play outsiders
who live a poverty-level existence in ramshackle abodes.
Both improvise daily amenities with the simplest components.
Both bring an "orphan" into their lives.   And, of course,
both experience the break-up of that relationship.

Beyond the superficial, the differences between the
two films are more striking than the similarities.   They are
no less sweeping than the differences between the Elf and the
Tramp.   The Elf is an outsider by ostracism; the Tramp, by
choice.   The Tramp shows repeatedly that he can master any
skill, if he has the desire.   The Elf has the desire but not
the ability.   Though they might perform similar tasks (both
played soldiers, street-cleaners, cops) they used those situations as mere departure points to mold their individuality.
Whatever Langdon may have borrowed from Chaplin, he made
his own. [7]

The focus of THE KID is the relationship between the
Tramp and the orphan.   In THREE'S A CROWD, the important thing (as always) is the ripple-effect of external events
on Harry's psyche.   The emblematic shot of THE KID is a
two-shot; the equivalent in the Langdon film is a close-up of
Harry's face.

He never truly engages the girl in an exchange of
feelings, as the Tramp does with the Kid.   His love is never
expressed.   The pathos is strictly derived from the Elf's enforced isolation, rather than the sundering of a formed connection between persons.   THE KID is about the experience
of loving; THREE'S A CROWD is about the need for love.

The most obvious difference is apparent when the central relationships are threatened. The most dramatic moment in THE KID (certainly the best known) occurs when social workers try to take the Kid from Charlie. The sequence is emotionally devastating, right up through the Tramp's swashbuckling rescue across the rooftops. The corresponding scene in THREE'S A CROWD is perhaps the most understated moment in the entire film. Where Chaplin was bombastic, Langdon was reserved. His acting in this scene is superb. Although the reunited lovers occupy the foreground, the viewer's eyes are riveted on the Elf. His faint-hearted attempts to smile, his slight nod as if he approves of the reunion, all hold back his real feelings. They are expressed with characteristic effortlessness: resignation, horror, depression.

The Elf had none of the pluck and resourcefulness of the Tramp, who one knew would survive simply because he was a "survivor." Without God on his side, pushing away obstacles and creating opportunities, Harry didn't stand a chance. A happy ending (as in THE KID) had no place in the new Langdon formula.

Recently, Marcel Marceau wrote:

> If you compare [Langdon] to Charlot, you will notice that Chaplin has revealed both sides of human nature: Joy and tragedy, which always will make of him a universal artist. In Harry Langdon, we see only one side of human fragility: a terrible loneliness and melancholy of a poor soul lost in a dark and wild world. [8]

Agee commented:

> It seemed as if Chaplin could do literally anything, on any instrument in the orchestra. Langdon had one queerly toned, unique little reed. But out of it he could get incredible melodies. [9]

In a way, the Langdon film can be seen as Harry's "answer" to the Tramp. They had frequently been compared, as in The New York Times: "Mr. Langdon is still Charles Spencer Chaplin's sincerest flatterer. His short coat reminds one of Chaplin, and now and again his footwork is like that of the great screen comedian."[10] THREE'S A CROWD puts that notion to rest. By choosing an ostensibly Chaplinesque story, their differences as screen clowns are set in bold

relief. Might not this have been Langdon's intention? The
possibility has almost never been considered.

* * *

Despite the film's conceptual and structural brilliance,
THREE'S A CROWD is a tragically flawed film. It is impossible to call it a masterpiece without conceding that it is
(almost equally) a failure. Deftly realized ideas are followed
by ill-advised artistic choices. Rarely have so many contradictory critical judgments been possible in the discussion
of a single comedy.

Gerald Mast wrote: "Langdon is trying to do something different and personal, reaching much further than
Capra tried to take him, but unfortunately without the stylis-
tic mastery or intellectual control."[11]

In a technical sense, the film betrayed Harry's obvious inexperience behind the camera. The editing is astonishingly clumsy at times. Matching shots do not match.
Scenes that should take one minute take three.

Harry stands on a chair to extinguish the street light
by his bed. For some reason there is a cut--the lamp has
gone dark--which should, but can't, match the previous action. The effect is jarring. Suddenly, the illusion is shattered by decidedly amateurish technique. Langdon chose to
shoot much of the film in long-held takes with a stationary
camera, which made cutting in the middle of scenes nearly
impossible. By 1927, audiences were used to smooth editing
and wouldn't overlook this kind of awkward sleight-of-hand.

More than any other factor, Langdon's new slower pace
doomed THREE'S A CROWD as a successful popular entertainment. Comedy depends on the release of dramatic tension to
generate laughter. When that tension is allowed to dissipate,
perfectly good comic ideas fall flat. Harry's discovery of
the baby clothes is a good example. There is nothing wrong
with the concept of the gag. Langdon had built a career reacting to the unexpected. The execution of the gag is simply
too slow. Even comic morons were expected to react with
more dispatch. Harry had pushed the limits too far.

Even when the gags were poorly executed, they were
often based on a solid conceptual framework. Underneath
the edge of the rug in Harry's shack is a trapdoor. In his

haste, he forgets to shut it. When he returns home later,
he steps on the supposedly solid rug and slips through the
trapdoor, saved only by grabbing the portion of the rug that
slips through with him. The slippage of the rug stops when
the trapdoor flips shut, wedged tightly by Harry's weight.
Every time he clambers up the rug and tries to get inside,
he flips up the trapdoor and the rug slips down further, taking him with it.

As a thrill sequence, it is substandard. It has nothing to do with the story. No attempt was made to indicate
that it is actually Langdon (and not a stunt man) in jeopardy,
so the viewer feels very little fear. The topper consists of
nothing more exciting than Harry falling, his descent cushioned
when he crashes through the roof of his employer's truck.

Yet, it is exceptional in two ways. First, it graphi-
cally demonstrates that even solid reality can be deceptive,
when Langdon first slips through the "floor." Second, the
agony of Harry's no-win universe becomes frighteningly apparent when all his efforts to save himself contain built-in
failure. Though the sequence is irrelevant to the story in a
narrative sense, it does re-state the film's theme. Unfortunately, it is tedious and not funny.

The early previews in July and August of 1927 warned
Langdon, Ripley, and the First National executives that
THREE'S A CROWD was in serious trouble. Audiences, at
first enthusiastic in their reception--expecting (why not?)
comedy of the calibre of THE STRONG MAN--grew bored
during the tender scenes and found few of the gags amusing.

The film was still unfinished. Langdon tried an innovative experiment with the editing, according to Tom Waller
in Motion Picture Magazine. [12] He shot approximately 200,000
feet of film (twice as much as Capra did for LONG PANTS)
and used the audience reaction (or lack of it) at the first
sneak previews to help him shape the finished film. Most
silent clowns used previews to fine tune their comedies, but
none as extensively as Langdon did with THREE'S A CROWD.

He made several adjustments. He returned to the
United Lot in Burbank and shot additional footage. No com-
prehensive record of all the changes has come to light, but
a few facts can be pieced together. He beefed up his own
scenes in the beginning portions. There were cuts. An
early ad mentions a scene where a fat lady pursues Harry,

with amorous intent; another has the Elf frozen into a huge,
solid block of ice, with only his head protruding. Neither
sequence appears in the completed film, and it is not known
if they were even filmed. The advance publicity for many
motion pictures is prepared from the shooting script, a risky
matter with everchanging comedy scenarios.

The film lacked a really big finish, so Harry filmed
the accidental destruction of the Swami's storefront, and the
earlier palm-reading scene as the "plant." THREE'S A
CROWD had originally ended with Harry running up the stairway to his shack, having "blown out" all the streetlights.
This was apparently thought to be too gently comic, and the
new "boffo" ending was added.

Langdon's tinkering couldn't salvage the film, which
was already far over budget. (To put that into perspective,
Chaplin spent five times as much--$900,000--on THE CIRCUS,
which premiered shortly after the Langdon film.) Knowing it
still had problems, Langdon was forced to release it without
further changes.

THREE'S A CROWD was condemned by the same critics who had encouraged him to experiment. Mordaunt Hall
sounded a familiar theme: "It happens only too often ... that
the bright bits are followed by a barrage of buffoonery that
has about as much right in the narrative as a chimney sweep
would have in a flour mill."[13]

Photoplay was worse:

> Harry Langdon reaches for the moon in this and
> grasps--a feeble glow-worm. He has tried to stuff
> the plots of Chaplin's THE KID and Charlie Ray's
> THE GIRL I LOVED into one picture. The result
> is an absurd, unbelievable story. To top the blun-
> der, he makes you wade through thick layers of
> oleomargarine pathos to get at the comedy. We
> like Harry Langdon and hate to hear the sound of
> his flops. May his next be louder and funnier.[14]

The commercial failure of his first film without Frank
Capra was an embarrassing and professionally devastating
comedown for Harry Langdon. Just six months before, he
had been behind only Chaplin and Lloyd in overall popularity,
with two successful features in release. Now his new picture, on which he had staked much of his reputation, was
either rejected or ignored.

Just three months after the release of THREE'S A CROWD, Langdon wrote:

> There are few more tragic businesses in the world than the making of funny pictures. There is the tragedy, for example, of working for weeks, sometimes months, on a sequence, only to find that it fails to evolve even a ripple from the audience. The producer and the star often find that their most cherished material is not funny when transmitted to the screen and the result is a tragedy not only for the audience, but for the makers of the picture. [15]

NOTES

1. Theatre Magazine, December 1927, p. 22.
2. First National press release, April 15, 1926.
3. The Crazy Mirror, p. 92.
4. The New York Times, March 29, 1927.
5. McCabe, John. Mr. Laurel and Mr. Hardy, p. 158.
6. The Silent Clowns, p. 282.
7. Chaplin's use of a blind girl in CITY LIGHTS (1931) could just as easily be called an imitation of Langdon's THE STRONG MAN (1926).
8. Letter to the author, June 19, 1980.
9. Life Magazine, September 5, 1949, p. 80.
10. The New York Times, March 29, 1927.
11. The Comic Mind, p. 176.
12. August 13, 1927.
13. The New York Times, October 3, 1927.
14. Photoplay, October 1927, p. 127.
15. Theatre Magazine, December 1927, p. 22.

Chapter Eleven: THE LOST CAUSE

> "The oddest thing about this whole funny
> business is that the public really wants
> to laugh, but it's the hardest thing in the
> world to make them do it."
> --Harry Langdon[1]

Until the release of THREE'S A CROWD, Langdon had hardly
considered the possibility that his name on a theater marquis
might not guarantee a healthy box-office return. Not that his
first self-directed film was a total bust: it did marginal business in some markets, particularly in Europe where Harry
had a large following, and the Pierrot (sad clown) was a respected tradition. But Langdon had been riding high for
nearly three years, with scarcely a bad review to his name.
The critical slaps left him in a state near shock.

He had little time to ponder the reasons why THREE'S
A CROWD failed to please on a widespread scale. He did
not have the freedom to sit back for a few months and get
his bearings. His contract with First National, which had
originally seemed so serendipitous, allowed him scant recov-
ery time between pictures. The "product" had to be produced
and delivered without delay.

Most of the other major comedians had a much looser
schedule. After Harold Lloyd moved to Paramount, he produced just one feature comedy per year. He knew that increased output would require that standards be lowered.
Charlie Chaplin, mindful of the high expectations of his public,

took as much time as he wanted. His later films appeared
at three-year intervals. Harry had a mere six months to
turn over a finished film to First National. Story ideas in
a similar vein as THREE'S A CROWD, which had seemed
quite viable as follow-ups to that film, were quickly jettisoned
when the critics condemned Langdon's use of pathos and tragedy. Obviously, a new approach was needed.

Logic might have dictated that Harry hire an experienced director to give his fifth feature a firmer cinematic
hand. But the budget for THREE'S A CROWD had exceeded
its limit so much that money was tight on the follow-up, and
Langdon needed no extra salary to direct. Besides, his ego
was pricked by those who said he could not direct. With one
film behind him, Harry was determined to prove the naysayers
wrong.

The pressure on the comedian was enormous. He had
to restore his own tarnished artistic credibility, and it was
imperative that he make a commercially successful picture.
One flop could easily (he hoped) be forgotten. Two failures
might seriously jeopardize his career. When Photoplay suggested: "May his next be louder and funnier," Harry took
heed.

Langdon and Ripley (with gag men Clarence Hennecke,
Robert Eddy, and Harry McCoy) concocted what they felt
would be a surefire laugh-maker. Harry was cast in the
role of THE CHASER, slang for an inveterate womanizer.
At least his wife (Gladys McConnell) and mother-in-law (Helen
Hayward) are convinced of his persistent infidelity.

The film opens with Harry's domestic double-threat
furiously awaiting the return of the tardy husband. When he
finally telephones, they take turns dispensing verbal abuse.
On the other end of the line, Harry (calling from a local
speakeasy) sits motionless in a chair, the receiver up to
one ear.

He listens for a short time, then moves the receiver
away, eventually holding it at arm's length. He seems frozen
with dread, knowing they won't believe that he is at a lodge
meeting (his usual alibi). Who could blame the little guy for
seeking respite from these twin harpies?

The Elf's alternatives are equally unpleasant: a gun-
fight at the speakeasy or fireworks at home. He chooses

the latter, hoping his lodge story will stick. He enters his
living room cautiously, smiling ruefully, and flipping his little wave.

This time, his punishment is more severe than he had
imagined. His wife takes him to court, seeking a divorce,
but an apparently demented judge (Charles Thurston) decides
to make an example of Harry and renders a freak decision:
Harry must wear skirts and assume his wife's duties in the
home for thirty days or go to jail. (His wife will take Harry's
place in the office for the same period of time.) She happily
accepts the decision, hoping Harry will be taught a good lesson.

He first appears in skirts the next morning, as he
emerges from his backyard chicken coop. His outfit stops
short of complete drag, however. He still wears his hat
and slapshoes. In a skirt and sweater, Harry looks like a
child victim of some variant of sexual pervert. His face
radiates extreme humiliation and resignation. Even Harry's
repressive mother in LONG PANTS would not have gone this
far. The recurring Langdon motif of sexual role reversal
(introduced in PICKING PEACHES) has led to this nightmarish
experience for the Little Elf.

Harry has failed to find any eggs for his wife's breakfast. Dressed in a suit and tie (but wearing a skirt rather
than pants), she sits at the breakfast table, pounding her
fists. She must have her eggs! He meekly returns to the
backyard to ponder the problem.

He puts a hen on his frying pan and waits. He makes
a feeble little "well--come on!" gesture. Nothing happens.
He picks up the chicken, holds it next to his ear, and shakes
it. The results are inconclusive. He holds the chicken
firmly in both hands and tries to squeeze an egg out of it.
Still nothing.

Meanwhile, a second chicken has produced an egg
underneath Harry's squatting body. He stands up and sees
it. He blinks slowly--several times. It is still there. He
bends closer to examine it, scratching his head. Could he
have actually laid that egg himself? The possibility causes
Harry to react with shame, as he furtively hides the egg in
the bushes and kicks dirt over it. Eventually, the chickens
comply and Harry has a "good" egg to prepare ... although
he loses it in the folds of his skirt before it can reach his
skillet.

Forced to wear skirts, Harry contemplates suicide in THE CHASER (First National, 1928). (The Museum of Modern Art, New York City)

In the course of his wifely domestic chores, the Elf
must fend off a pass from a salesman.   When the iceman
also pecks him on the cheek, even Little Harry has reached
his limit.   Suicide is his only escape from this domestic
Hell.   "No man can stand to wear skirts," he writes in his
farewell note.   That the kitchen is about to become an arena
of death is just one interesting aspect of Langdon's study of
sexual roles.

First he tries using a large pistol to end his life.
One problem: where to point it so that the pain will be minimized.   His head?   His heart?   His foot?   Wavering indecisively, he finds a tiny revolver, which is more to his liking (as if a smaller weapon will make the job easier).   As
he points the weapon at his head, his eyes bulge out and his
whole body shakes.   Naturally, he has inadvertently selected
a squirt gun.

Next he tries poison.   From the cabinet, he produces
all manner of toxic substances, but after mixing them together
in a glass, he fumbles again.   Instead, he drinks a large
glass of castor oil.   The horrible taste causes not only his
cheek to puff but his lower lip to pull down and sideways in
a comic grimace.   He lies down on the kitchen floor to wait
stoically for the end.   The camera holds the shot for a long
time.   Suddenly he sits bolt upright, jumps to his feet, and
runs upstairs.   The "poison" has had its effect.

Now the film's mood lifts.   Harry's lodge buddy (Bud
Jamison) convinces him to escape his prison for an afternoon
of fun.   Soon they stumble upon a bevy of Sennett-like bathing
girls at a beach.   His friend quickly mingles, but Harry in-
securely hangs back.

He gets an idea.   Moments later, Harry returns wearing his lodge uniform (which he had brought along for his
alibi).   The Napoleonic hat sports a huge feathery plume, and
the coat has epaulets and shiny buttons.   It is a shade too
big for Harry, but he still relies on the uniform to make him
seem a dashing, romantic lover (echoing the fantasy sequence
in LONG PANTS).

Remaining several yards from the girls, his sole over-
ture consists of a few squirty winks.   Amazingly, one of the
girls notices him.   She is mesmerized by this strikingly hand-
some apparition and moves toward him as if in a trance.   In
a spoof of Valentino, Harry's magnetic charm casts a spell
over the beautiful girl.

She puts her arms around him, hangs on his shoulder. He stands immobile, facing the camera, patting her on the back with a stubby hand. She pulls closer and kisses him. The effect is devastating--for her. She swoons and sinks slowly to the ground in a dead faint.

His confidence bolstered by this unexpected conquest, Harry grows bolder. He spots a spinsterish school-marm type standing near a picnic table. Harry comes up behind her and abruptly swings around into her line of vision. She stares mutely up at him (his back is now to the camera) and falls under his spell. Harry very deliberately places his hands on either side of her face and kisses her emphatically. Within seconds she, too, is lying on the ground in disarray, another victim of the Elf's inexplicable sensual power.

Thinking her husband has actually committed suicide, Harry's wife (who has brought her bridge club home to see how she dominates her husband) sits on a kitchen chair and sobs uncontrollably. Her mascara smears down her face as she cries. The image perfectly suits her wretched realization of the damage that she has done to Harry.

The final scene of THE CHASER depicts Harry's reconciliation with his wife. At first, she confesses her sorrow to what she thinks is Harry's ghost. Actually, it is Harry himself, completely coated with white cornstarch (the result of a kitchen accident). He greets her abject apology with a look of extreme skepticism. The film ends as it began, with the title: "In the beginning God created man. A little later on, He created woman. "

*   *   *

Langdon's fifth independent feature is not without several weaknesses, especially in comparison to the consistently high standards of his first three First National pictures. The most seriously flawed aspect is the script. In his review of THE CHASER, Mordaunt Hall wrote: "The story ... is seldom plausible and not often funny. [The gags] need more raison d'etre than they have in this production. "[2]

The relative importance of plausibility in a comedy can be debated, but Hall was quite correct to point out that Langdon (and his writing staff) had reached too far for certain gags, apparently unable to resist a funny idea. The film's central premise (the judge's freak decision) is not a bad comedy springboard, but if one values plausibility, it falls wide of

THE CHASER (First National, 1928).   (Michael Copner
Collection)

the mark.   One cannot imagine that situation occurring in
the real world.

Equally implausible are some of the smaller gags.
On the edge of a golf course, Harry watches with mounting
horror as the patch of grass in front of a nearby gravestone
begins moving, as if the body buried beneath has come to
life.   What could be the explanation?   A small dog has bur-
rowed into a gopher hole and is digging underneath the turf.
The gravestone is actually some sort of advertisement.   The
writers were grasping at straws.   (The same sort of gag had
marred a sequence in LONG PANTS.   When Harry loses his
gun in the leaves, during his frustrated attempt to shoot
Priscilla, he picks up what he thinks is the gun.   It is a gun-
shaped stick that is tied to a rope that is attached to a horse.
The horse--nowhere in sight moments before--suddenly bolts,
knocking Harry to the ground.)

Perhaps more serious were certain gags that violated
Langdon's well-established elfin character.   When a lecherous
salesman pecks him on the cheek, mistaking him for a house-
wife (unbelievable in itself) Harry fails to call upon his regular lexicon of hesitant, confused gestures.   Instead, he becomes enraged, tosses a chamber pot after the man (which
lands over his head) and shatters the pot with a brick.   Simple anger did not go down well with audiences conditioned to
Harry's legendary meekness.

Even the Valentino spoof, the prime set-piece of THE
CHASER, pushes the Elf onto shaky ground.   The sequence
superficially imitates Harry's sexual potency in the Sennett
three-reeler, SOLDIER MAN.   But that had been a dream.
In real life, Harry's sensual power doesn't make sense.

Other gags might be considered in poor taste.   The
anal humor would not appeal to everyone.   When Harry "lays
an egg" or violently reacts to castor oil, a certain segment
of the public would find the images distasteful.

THE CHASER is, quite obviously, misogynic in the
extreme.   Langdon's wife in SATURDAY AFTERNOON had
been a bitch, but her part was relatively small.   In the expanded version of that role, Gladys McConnell plays a more
integral part in the story.   She approves of Harry's punishment and relishes bragging to her friends: "See how I drive
my husband!"   It is nearly impossible to imagine how she

could have married him in the first place.   Harry's uncomplimentary portrayal of women could not have pleased his
many female fans.

His personal life was in turmoil and may have contributed to this attitude.   Rose and Harry had separated.
Around the time of the completion of THE CHASER, she
charged him with cruelty and desertion, and asked for
$70,000 in alimony.   Later, Harry lamented: "I have been
married twice, and I have learned that women just must
quarrel.   Women are like that.   I don't feel like making an
audience laugh after I have had a quarrel with a woman.   In
order to be a good comedian I must escape the tragedy of
marriage. "[3]

THE CHASER is more than a longer version of Harry's
highly successful Sennett short comedy, SATURDAY AFTER-
NOON.   As in the first film, the Elf steps out with his mash-
er friend for a girl-chasing spree, after being harangued by
his domineering wife.   But Langdon could not have copied
the same ebullient mood and style of SATURDAY AFTERNOON,
even if he had tried.

Each of his feature comedies had charted a distinct
progression in the Elf's journey from innocence to experience.
Although THE CHASER borrowed specific ideas from several
earlier films (the tiny revolver from PLAIN CLOTHES, the
broken steering wheel from HIS MARRIAGE WOW, the basic
plot from SATURDAY AFTERNOON), they now suggest a
mixed-up interior hallucination.   Shattered by the conclusion
of THREE'S A CROWD, the Little Elf now had descended into
delirium and even insanity.   The nightmarish quality of the
scenario and imagery further evoke the connection with Harry's
unconscious mind.   THE CHASER can be seen as a dream
within a dream.

It is as if Harry's mind is shifting over past events,
filtering them through a new, highly disturbed awareness.
When his runaway car teeters on the brink of a cliff, echoing
the scene in TRAMP, TRAMP, TRAMP where he hangs on a
fence, the resolution is the same: the "sheer cliff" turns
into a far more manageable steep incline.   Trapped in the
careening vehicle, Harry's face and hands convey a horror
of speeding out of control that transcends the specifics of the
situation.

In addition to the aspects of psychological horror and

sexual abberation, THE CHASER displays several other strong
points. The common view of Harry Langdon as a director
was expressed in The Film Mercury: "The trouble is that
he has grown self-conscious, not as an actor, but as a director. Even though the star wants to be a tragic figure,
he could never have imagined how really tragic he is in THE
CHASER."[4] A careful study of the film belies that point of
view.

Langdon had learned much during the making of
THREE'S A CROWD, and it showed in THE CHASER. Kevin
Brownlow wrote: "It establishes him, in retrospect at least,
as an excellent comedy director--not in the Capra class, but
certainly as good as Edwards."[5] Durgnat also found much
to admire: "In THE CHASER ... some elaborate tracking
shots, of rare formal beauty, astonishingly anticipate Renoir's
BOUDO SAUVE DES EAUX. Keaton's sense of railroad rhy-
thms is paralleled by Langdon's flair for slow, wavering
movements, with their hallucinatory poetry."[6] As Harry
walks purposefully through his house, the camera dollies
alongside, passing through breakaway walls.

Langdon did make one glaring editing mistake. The
long shot of Harry on the floor waiting for the "poison" to
take effect is marred by a needless close-up of his upper
body. Since the pay-off depends on holding that single long
shot for an audacious length of time, Harry had undercut his
own gag. In the main, however, THE CHASER is edited
smoothly and the pacing (with one or two minor exceptions)
is suitable to a comedy.

The film contains several masterfully elaborate sequences which nearly equal the level of gag invention in THE
STRONG MAN and LONG PANTS. The chicken-and-egg routine is quite clever and well-developed, and the Valentino
spoof is hilarious and charming.

The actor/comedian was in top form. As Harry listens to his wife's harangue in the opening scene, his babyish
blankness emanates more from his consciousness at that moment than any awareness of his behavior or environment.
His responses had deepened. An aura of futility adds a som-
ber tinge to his elfin character.

Harry has learned that even inanimate objects like a
telephone can be conductors of pain. It is as if the physical
world conspires against him. He had always had difficulty

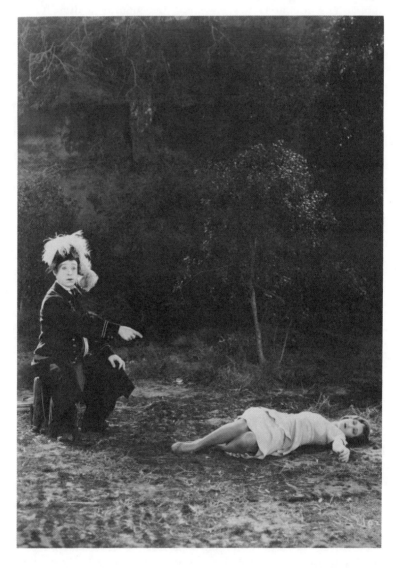

"All I did was kiss her!" remarks Harry in THE CHASER
(First National, 1928). (The Museum of Modern Art, New
York City)

relating to his own body, but in the Capra period, he had
been trying to grow into his role as an adult in society.   In
THE CHASER, one has the impression that Harry would
rather escape his body altogether, for he finds little pleasure in that association.   His body is now part of the solid
reality that had mocked him in THREE'S A CROWD.

All this Langdon somehow conveys in his first minute
on the screen, through his posture, his facial expression,
and a few flighty movements.   His pantomime had become,
in just three years, the very essence of minimalistic expression, almost as though he could communicate by osmosis.
Langdon doing (seemingly) nothing could be eloquent.

THE CHASER remains, on balance, an entertaining
and challenging film.   Harry had succeeded in constructing
an excellent showcase for his talents, and probably felt reasonably confident that it would reassert his prominence as a
major laugh-maker.   There had been no evidence that his
public was through with him.

After all, he was still Harry Langdon.   His ability
as a screen farceur was undiminished.   As he prepared THE
CHASER for its premiere (February 12, 1928), Langdon had
no way of knowing that a number of factors were converging
that would, in effect, deny him a fair shot at a comeback.
If his ascension was partly due to fortuitous timing, his decline would be even more intimately affected by film trends
in late 1927 and 1928.   THREE'S A CROWD had failed at the
worst possible time.

*   *   *

When THE CHASER was released, a public that might have
overlooked nominal weaknesses in his earlier work now
greeted him with nearly total indifference.   Sound had finally
come to the film medium.

Of course, early forms of synchronized sound had accompanied a few films before the turn of the century, but it
wasn't until the advent of commercial radio that anyone in
Hollywood became interested in changing the silent tradition.
The slump in profits in the middle-to-late 1920's gave the
Warner Bros.' new sound-on-disc system the impetus it
needed; its first real test occurred with the premiere of
Warner's DON JUAN on June 4, 1926.   The film contained
no spoken dialogue, but the lush soundtrack (and some sound

effects) were synchronized. Accompanying the Barrymore
vehicle was almost an hour of shorts of major entertainers
of the day, both popular and serious. Audiences were
stunned. This milestone event took place only two months
after TRAMP, TRAMP, TRAMP was released. Even then,
Harry was living on borrowed time.

With various delays due to technical problems, silent
films held their own against the talkie revolution for longer
than most realize. The initial euphoria soon wore off by
the spring of 1927, until Fox released its first Movietone
newsreels, which had sound accompanying a real event (Lind-
bergh's historic flight) instead of a stage show inside a studio.
Again the public and film people became excited when they
sensed the real potential of talking pictures. And the delay
had given Langdon a chance to have big hits with THE
STRONG MAN and LONG PANTS.

Harry might have handily weathered the electrifying
success of THE JAZZ SINGER on October 6, 1927, had
THREE'S A CROWD (released a scant month before) been a
resounding hit. But when Langdon's bubble burst, the talkie
change-over severely handicapped his chances of regaining
his momentum.

Not that Harry was being pressured to speak onscreen.
Silent films continued for two more years, while theaters
across the country scrambled to install expensive sound
equipment. But the real excitement increasingly centered on
the talking pictures; it was an uphill battle to renew interest
in an unassuming nebbish like Langdon, when everyone was
going wild for the brassy, dynamic Jolson.

The release of Chaplin's new silent comedy, THE
CIRCUS (January 1928), may also have dampened Harry's
comeback chances. To some extent, Langdon had filled in
the gap as a sort of surrogate-Tramp during Charlie's three-
year absence from the screen. The critics often hailed
Harry as a potential threat to Chaplin's own popularity. But
with Langdon's career on the skids, Chaplin's film quickly
reasserted his position in the industry (never in serious
doubt) and may have diminished interest in a comeback for
the Little Elf.

More than any of the top four silent clowns, Langdon's
career bore the earmarks of a fad. His talent was authentic,
but his rise to fame was so fast that one suspects he was

riding partially on a convenient trend in popular taste. For
a brief period of time his absurd child/man persona was the
rage. When tastes shifted, Langdon's fortunes sagged. The
New York Times adequately summed up the new sentiments:
"Stupidity on the part of a character does not necessarily
make him a comic genius. Spectators get tired of laughing
at a character who is obviously not quite right in his mind."

Fads are characterized by a sudden explosive emergence, followed by over-saturation, and a fast decline. Langdon probably came dangerously close to the point of over-
saturation during the spring of 1927. It wasn't his fault.
Mack Sennett released HIS FIRST FLAME as a feature film
with no regard for how it might adversely affect Harry's
career. LONG PANTS had only been out one month, and
Langdon had rarely been off the screen since he first arrived at Mack Sennett Studios. The failure of THREE'S A
CROWD completed the pattern.

One strange aspect of a fad is the public's inordinate
resentment toward the person it has so recently idolized,
after the initial excitement is over. They are perhaps
slightly chagrined by their own over-enthusiasm. Though
difficult to prove, the scathing quality of the reviews and
the suddenness of Langdon's rejection seem to indicate that
a Langdon backlash did happen.

That backlash may have been partially caused by
Harry's lack of savvy in handling the press. He took his
honeymoon with the press corps for granted. What he may
not have understood was that once a star was established,
he or she was considered fair game. Instead of catering to
the reporters, Langdon irritated them and held them at a
distance by hiring several personal assistants. Some of
them resembled (and were, more or less) bodyguards.

Taken individually, these theories are perhaps too
pat, and more than a little simplistic. Langdon had too
much talent to be strictly a faddist item. He was not widely
perceived to be a substitute Chaplin. Talking pictures did
not firmly take over until 1929 and even 1930. The press
could not "break" a star that the public still adored. But
taken together, these forces could, and did, stack the odds
heavily against the success of THE CHASER.

First National made very little effort to publicize and
promote the film. THREE'S A CROWD had created a quick

rift between the star and the money men. By the time the
following film was nearing completion, the industry papers
were reporting that Langdon would not renew his contract
with First National. While it is unlikely that the company
would deliberately sabotage their own film, their half-hearted
release of THE CHASER amounted to the same thing.

The critics loathed the new Langdon film. Richard
Watts, Jr. of the New York Tribune wrote:

> It was not so long ago that a number of us were
> heralding Mr. Langdon ... as virtually the legiti-
> mate successor of the mighty Mr. Chaplin. Today,
> unfortunately, we are forced to rush about in quest
> of alibis for our former ecstasy. [7]

A. J. in Morning World commented:

> The audience which attended this showing ... did
> not receive [THE CHASER] kindly. One spectator
> was heard to liken Mr. Langdon's facial expres-
> sions to a blank and unintelligent look of a two-
> year-old, while others near an exit were stepping
> out into the cool air. [8]

THE CHASER made even less money than THREE'S
A CROWD. Photoplay accurately predicted that it spelled
Langdon's "doom as a leader in the screen comedy field."
Harry Langdon was now a has-been.

NOTES

1. Photoplay, June 1925, p. 126.
2. The New York Times, April 10, 1928.
3. New York American, October 13, 1931.
4. The Film Mercury, April 20, 1928.
5. The Parade's Gone By, p. 40.
6. The Crazy Mirror, p. 91.
7. The Film Mercury summary, April 20, 1928, p. 14.
8. Ibid.

Chapter Twelve: HEART TROUBLE

Tragically, Langdon's final film for First National has been lost. No copy has survived on any gauge film stock, and the negative seems to have vanished. HEART TROUBLE has not been seen since its initial release on October 2, 1928. Evidence indicates that it was barely seen, even then.

The year 1928 was a frantic one for the American film industry. It looked like talkies were going to save the studios from their financial doldrums. The sensational grosses of THE JAZZ SINGER (and virtually every other film with synchronized sound) made believers of the most stubborn studio bosses. They entered into a sometimes chaotic competition to outdo each other, pushing each new release a step closer to full realization of the new medium's potential.

Films like THE LIGHTS OF NEW YORK and IN OLD ARIZONA advanced the art, but fell short of accomplishing a truly comfortable marriage of image and sound. Still, they were good enough to put to rest the notion that talkies were just a fad. By the end of the year, almost everyone in films admitted that talking pictures had come to stay.

While most of the stories in the trade papers discussed talkies, silent films comprised a sizeable segment of the new studio releases. Key silents of 1928 were THE CROWD, OUR DANCING DAUGHTERS, THE CIRCUS, THE TEMPEST, SADIE THOMPSON, and THE WIND.

No major stars spoke on screen that year, including the four great silent clowns. Chaplin's THE CIRCUS, Lloyd's

HEART TROUBLE, with Doris Dawson (First National, 1928).
(Academy Collection)

SPEEDY, and Keaton's STEAMBOAT BILL JR. and THE
CAMERAMAN stayed with the pantomime tradition, as did
Langdon's last two independent features, THE CHASER and
HEART TROUBLE.

All but the most loved and firmly established silent
stars were on shaky ground. If a star had recently faltered
at the box-office, as Harry had, his or her films tended to
be rush-released. This may have been particularly true at
First National, since the company was taken over by Warner
Bros. (which had introduced Vitaphone sound-on-disc) in

HEART TROUBLE (First National, 1928).   (Wayne Powers
Collection)

September of 1928.   This meant that the chain of theaters
that made up the organization now had to undergo the costly
conversion for the showing of talkies, especially if they were
to reap the staggering profits of Jolson's follow-up to THE
JAZZ SINGER, entitled THE SINGING FOOL.   The second
Jolson film was released with spectacular fanfare on September 19, 1928.   Two weeks later, Harry's HEART TROUBLE
was ignominiously premiered (if that is the proper word) on
a double bill for one day only at the Loew's Theater in New
York City.

     This kind of shabby treatment not only indicated a
singular lack of confidence from First National, but may also
have resulted from the cost-cutting campaign of Warner Bros.
Shortly after their takeover, they trimmed a hundred employ-
ees from the staff of their new subsidiary.   The remaining
staff had to give their attention to "specials" and talkies.
True, HEART TROUBLE represented a $150,000 investment,
but Warners could not have looked kindly on spending good
money after bad, when the public had registered no interest
in THE CHASER.   Promotion and advertising were minimal.

     It wasn't just Harry's films that were shunted aside.
Indeed, of the (approximately) 6,000 known American feature
films made in the period between 1921 and 1930, only about
25 percent are known to survive, with a surprisingly large
number missing from the late 1920's.   Lawrence Karr of the
American Film Institute wrote that HEART TROUBLE "was
released during the transition to sound, which may have contributed to its box-office performance.   This certainly has
contributed to its disappearance."[1]

     With no monetary advantage to storing the prints of
HEART TROUBLE, a thoughtless studio employee probably
ordered their destruction.   Prints to "dead" films (thought
to have no further commercial value) were often sold for
their residual silver content.

     Very little is known about Langdon's last feature-length
silent.   Harry starred and directed, of course.   Arthur Ripley wrote the story, and Gordon Bradford composed the titles.
It was the shortest of the First Nationals, with a running time
of 58 minutes.   The cast included Doris Dawson as Harry's
girl, and Madge Hunt, Lionel Belmore, Bud Jamison, Mark
Hamilton, and Nelson McDowell.

     The plot was a variation on the situation that frequently

HEART TROUBLE (First National, 1928).   (The Museum of
Modern Art, New York City)

motivated comics of that era: an ordeal reluctantly under-
taken in order to win the girl's affections. Keaton had exploited this plot in COLLEGE, COPS, THE GENERAL and
others; Langdon himself had tried it on in FEET OF MUD
(1924), when he swept streets to garner the approval of
Natalie Kingston's father.

Of the story, Variety summarized:

> A novel angle on conscription during the war, with
> a small-town locale and with Langdon in one of his
> regular moron roles, is used. Failing to get into
> the Army after pestering a recruiting Colonel,
> Harry, through a coincidence, saves that official's
> life and blows up an enemy ammunitions depot. [2]

Harold Truscott, the British writer who claims to have
seen HEART TROUBLE twelve times (upon its British release)
wrote:

> In some ways, both THREE'S A CROWD and THE
> CHASER ... are psychological horror films. It is
> not so much horror that haunts [HEART TROUBLE]
> as a lingering regret for chances missed, coupled
> with the thought, which is behind much of the ac-
> tion, that if it were not for the girl it wouldn't be
> worth the effort anyway.
>   Langdon's presentation of this double and contra-
> dictory state of mind is masterly, since it is con-
> veyed again with practically no dialogue [titles] and
> the very real unity of the film is in no way impaired
> when, having failed in all his deliberate attempts to
> enlist, he blunders by chance into a military plot
> and emerges triumphant--on the surface.
>   Naturally, his triumph is accidental and is not
> even particularly welcome to him. He keeps his
> girl, but the very last shot of Harry's face shows
> a deep and lingering doubt as to whether even she
> was worth it. [3]

Walter Kerr speaks of a minor legend that exists, to
the effect that HEART TROUBLE represented a "partial re-
covery" for Harry. Variety's very positive review further
supports this notion:

> It is one of the best of the few [Langdon] has made
> during the past two years. It can stand up without
> a supporting feature for a short run in any house.

HEART TROUBLE, with Doris Dawson (First National, 1928).
(The Museum of Modern Art, New York City)

> The comic does less of the emoting he gave way
> to in his last two.   He abandons to a great extent
> his ambition to be the complex of tradegienne [sic]
> and a comedian.   [HEART TROUBLE is] more com-
> pact and the story is more actionful.   That he is
> directing himself is less obvious.   The gags are
> not so numerous, but the ones used are good.

The film may have done quite well overseas.   Truscott added:

> I remember that in the town where I lived, Ilford,
> HEART TROUBLE was booked for a week and re-
> tained for three.   This extended run happened at

two different cinemas in Ilford at different times, each time for HEART TROUBLE, a three-week run each time. [4]

The possibility that HEART TROUBLE is a lost classic is supported by the barest evidence: the Variety review (and other scattered good notices), the memories of a Langdon fan (Truscott), Kerr's talk of a "small legend." Certainly if Langdon's use of the camera took a quantum leap between his first and second directing efforts, why not again on the occasion of his third? Variety's assertion that he moved away from pathos, back to gag comedy, indicates that Harry must have faced commercial considerations quite squarely.

Yet, all the omens are not so positive. Photoplay did not so much review HEART TROUBLE as ridicule it. "Just a lot of silly gags, no story and enough inane situations to spell the exit of Harry Langdon. It was his cue to give us a good picture. He didn't." Photoplay's assessment accurately reflects the extent of the public's rejection of Langdon's comedy.

Unfortunately, the possibility that HEART TROUBLE was a better film than THREE'S A CROWD or THE CHASER may remain problematical. As of this writing, the film is fifty-four years old. The average lifespan of chemically unstable nitrate film stock (the type used during this period) is forty to fifty years. After that time, the chances are that a print will have turned into a foul-smelling jelly. Eventually, it decomposes into dust.

Time is running out, but there is still hope. Surprising everyone, some nitrate stock has survived in good shape up to seventy years. The negative itself may come to light. Lawrence Karr admits:

It is quite possible that the film will eventually turn up. [but he adds:] The film was released by First National, which apparently had rather tight control over its distribution prints; we very seldom acquire First National films from private collectors, who would be our best hope for locating a copy.

The odds that HEART TROUBLE will be found are difficult to figure, but it is safe to say that, like the career of the man who made it, it is a definite long shot.

NOTES

1. Letter to the author, July 3, 1980.
2. Variety, October 10, 1928.
3. The Silent Picture, summer 1972, p. 14.
4. Ibid., p. 16.
5. Photoplay, November 1928, p. 111.

Chapter Thirteen: TOUGH LUCK

Shortly before the abbreviated premiere of HEART TROUBLE in New York, Photoplay published a lengthy interview with Mack Sennett.[1] The interviewer, novelist Theodore Dreiser, was clearly impressed with Sennett's charismatic personality and knowledge of the comedy business.

At one point in his musings, Sennett brought up Langdon, "Whom I consider the greatest of them all."

Stunned, Dreiser blurted: "Greater than Chaplin?"

"Yes, greater than Chaplin. Langdon suggests a kind of baby weakness that causes everybody to feel sorry for him and want to help him out. He's terribly funny to me."

Sennett might have been grinding his axe for Chaplin, but he had nothing to gain from supporting Langdon. In the autumn of 1928, fashionable commentary no longer compared Harry to Charlie. Three flops in a row had brought Langdon down hard.

His daily life took on some of the nightmarish quality of his later comedies. Harry's failure made headlines. He was still in the throes of a stormy divorce with his first wife, which didn't help the negative tone of his press coverage. Langdon came to epitomize squandered talent, a classic case of "too much, too fast." It is difficult to think of another major comedian who had fallen from grace that fast, that completely.

The Little Elf had never taken root like the Little
Tramp, but he had been in circulation long enough to make
an impact on a generation.   When his show-business fairy
tale turned sour, he didn't just disappear.   Thousands of
people read of his troubles.   Even when he was working and
pulling himself out of a hole, his legendary failure over-
shadowed his nova-like brilliance.

For a while, Harry's reverses left him devastated.
The extent of his depression is clearly visible in the por-
traits distributed by First National for HEART TROUBLE.
In one, a cigarette dangles from his mouth.   Gone is his
costume, his powdered face and his smile.   He wears a
dark business suit.

He looks fragile and hurt.   His eyes are cast down,
and have no luster.   In another, his eyes appeal directly to
the viewer.   In the soft focus, he looks as if he is fading
into a quicksand of shattered dreams.   The dream was over.
Or was it?   Harry assessed his situation.   Things could have
been worse.   Although his cash reserves were running low,
he was not completely broke.   Newspaper stories told of
Langdon pinning thousand dollar bills underneath furniture,
where Rose wouldn't find them.   Although his star-sized
lifestyle was quickly caving in, his credit was still good.

Supposedly, Harry was talking contract with United
Artists, a company partly owned by Charles Chaplin.   The
very idea of Langdon working for Chaplin was preposterous,
and may have been just wishful thinking on Harry's part.
Everyone knew that Langdon was (at least temporarily) box-
office poison.

Fortunately, Harry Langdon was something more than
just a movie actor.   If he couldn't make films, he would return to the vaudeville stage and make the film producers notice him.   He could command top dollar on the ailing Keith
circuit.

Variety entertainment was in its death throes by 1929.
Commercial radio had hit hard in the early twenties, and
talking pictures had ended all hope of a vaudeville revival.
Almost all outlets included films in their program.   It seemed
as if only the Palace in New York City (re-named the RKO
Palace) held firm.   The prestigious Palace could not be easily supplanted.

In this publicity photo for HEART TROUBLE (First National, 1928), Langdon's face reflected his tragic circumstances. (Michael Copner Collection)

Vaudevillians all speak of the Palace with awe. In
The Vaudevillians, Jack Haley remembered: "Only a vaudevillian who has trodden its stage ... can describe the anxi-
eties at the Palace." On March 17, 1929, the full-page ads
appeared in Variety: Langdon at the Palace for a solid month.

The act itself, a seventeen-minute parlor skit called
"The Messenger," was distinctly second-rate. Langdon played
a messenger boy who becomes the pawn in a game of spite
between a jealous wife and her philandering husband. Despite the inadequacies of the script (which Harry had written),
he "got over" with the crowd, but (as Variety observed):

> ... not before meeting more than one obstacle
> along the way. Langdon would have done vastly
> better by returning to his old and well-remembered
> auto skit. Langdon depended mostly on mugging
> and goof characterization and was far from him-
> self when struggling with an indifferent script. [2]

The New York Times agreed:

> The sketch in which he displays himself at the
> Palace does not show [his] gifts to best advantage,
> and certainly it could reasonably be expected to be
> a little funnier. [3]

Variety concluded:

> Following the full stage action, which was laughless
> but for Harry's facial business, Langdon appeared
> before the drape for five minutes of intimate talk
> and topped off with a comedy dance. That dance
> lasting about a minute brought more response than
> all of the preceeding seventeen minutes. [4]

The quality of the material did not seem to matter.
Langdon's run at Palace was a great personal success and
got him what he wanted: good press. Reporter Leonard
Hall described the first week of the engagement as "a roar-
ing, triumphant week, with the house jammed with Langdon
maniacs, a vicious sort of devotee, and yards of blazing
praise from press and public in the pews."[5] The Little Elf,
in his latest permutation, was (in Leonard Hall's opinion)
as great as ever.

The reporter Hall and the re-born vaudevillian sat in

a luxurious suite in the Warwick Hotel. Langdon wore a smoking jacket and his glasses. The two men looked out the window into sunny Central Park as they talked about the strange twist in Harry's career.

Hall asked what had happened at First National. What had gone wrong? "Tough luck," Langdon answered. He contended that the First National executives had cut his budgets and demanded that shooting be completed in six weeks. He seemed to concede the shortcomings of THREE'S A CROWD and THE CHASER, but wondered how anyone could have expected better under those stringent conditions.

Langdon was eager to send out positive signals. He was willing to adapt to the latest developments in movie comedy.

> I believe that the day of the long gag comedy, with the whole picture depending on the efforts of a starred comedian, is over. A kick in the pants isn't as funny as it was in 1910. The gag field has been worked bare.
> The story is the thing of today and tomorrow-- the laugh picture with a tale to tell. No living comic can carry the whole burden of a seven reel comedy and make it one long howl. No man can be that funny and live. He must have the help of a good story and two or three all-wool featured actors to help him play it. [6]

While excusing weaknesses in his own films, Langdon was also accurately predicting the shape of film comedy of the thirties. In a bid for mass commercial success, Irving Thalberg piloted the Marx Brothers to their biggest hit of all time. A NIGHT AT THE OPERA (1935) featured realistic actors (in a certain sense) and a love story. By 1940, only W. C. Fields and Laurel and Hardy continued to make episodic star-vehicle comedies, and their days were numbered.

Armed with these rather democratic views on the future of film comedy, and basking in the after glow of his (only slightly tarnished) run at the Palace, Harry headed back

[Opposite:] HOTTER THAN HOT (Hal Roach, 1929), with Thelma Todd (right). (The Museum of Modern Art, New York City)

to the film capital. Vaudeville had been a nice change-of-pace, and an efficient boost for his reputation, but it had been essentially a publicity stunt to help him return to his true calling.

Langdon's ploy worked. Hal Roach, the comedy producer who had first approached him in 1923 with a film deal, offered Harry a five-year contract for eight two-reel short comedies a year. The Langdon series would then be sold along with other Roach items like Laurel and Hardy, Charley Chase and Our Gang. The contracts were signed in late May 1929. Eight months after his debacle at First National, Harry was ready to begin shooting his first sound film.

*   *   *

Hal Roach was born in 1892, and grew up in Elmira, New York. At nineteen, he moved to California and held many odd jobs during the next two years. In 1913, he found himself working as an extra on a Universal western for five dollars a day. He quickly became an assistant director and then a director at Essanay studios, and befriended another young extra named Harold Lloyd. Soon, with the timely help of an inheritance, Roach formed his own company. Lloyd's first screen character, Willie Work, appeared in early Roach comedies.

Times were not always easy for the embryonic studio. Roach labored tirelessly for years trying to evolve successful series comedies. He signed Will Rogers in 1923 for a long-running series and lavished attention on Our Gang (where Frank Capra got his start as a gag man). By the time Langdon moved to the Sennett studio, Roach was moving up fast. The teaming of Stan Laurel and Oliver Hardy in 1927 pushed him to the front ranks of the comedy producers. Mack Sennett had become a crusty anachronism, an old-time mogul out of touch with audiences that had grown more sophisticated and demanding. Despite technical advances like Sennett Color, his films hadn't changed much since 1914. His reign as comedy king was over, and his mantle was assumed by Hal Roach.

Roach wore the crown with a disarming lack of arrogance and pretense. He was a benevolent, fatherly presence who genuinely loved comedy and felt that laughter could best be generated in a relaxed atmosphere. Sennett had often bullied his personnel, but Roach used soft-spoken persuasion.

THE BIG KICK (Hal Roach, 1930), with Nancy Dover. (The Museum of Modern Art, New York City)

As a result, the Roach lot in Culver City had a reputation as the friendliest lot in the business. His large stable
of comics and supporting players all spoke glowing of those
idyllic times in later interviews. Sometimes they would knock
off at three o'clock, other times they would willingly work
all night without extra pay. They were making people laugh,
that was all that mattered. If the major studio stars looked
down their noses at lowly Roach comedies, no one cared.

Harry Langdon's new comedy series was hailed with
considerable media fanfare. Roach announced that Langdon
was returning to two-reelers, his "first love"--the format
that had made him a star. HOTTER THAN HOT (1929), the
first Langdon film at Roach, was directed by Lewis Foster,
which augured well for Harry's talking debut. Foster had
successfully directed the first Laurel and Hardy talkie, UN-
ACCUSTOMED AS WE ARE (1929), and ranked as an experienced hand in the new sound medium. Excellent support was
provided in the first film (and several others) by a vivacious
blond who would soon become the Queen of the Roach lot.
Thelma Todd, a beauty-contest winner, possessed a vivid
comedy style that led her to ably support the Marx Brothers
in HORSE FEATHERS (1932) before her tragic murder/suicide
in 1935.

THE SHRIMP (1930) typifies the strengths and weaknesses of Langdon's Roach series. It was directed by Charley Rogers, a British writer/director who worked often with
Laurel and Hardy, and would team up with Harry onscreen
in later years. The whimsical "Pop! Goes the Weasel" was
adopted for Langdon's theme song.

His entrance is cleverly accomplished. The first shot
established the setting as a large boarding house. Various
residents arrive downstairs for breakfast. They are all stock
comic types: the burly bully, his brassy girlfriend (Todd),
the lazy owner and his overworked wife. Someone asks:
"Say, has anyone seen the shrimp?"

Cut to an upstairs door. Fumbling sounds emanate
from behind the door. It sounds as if someone is unlocking
the door from the other side. Suddenly, Harry pops into
view. His theme music plays on the soundtrack. He looks

[Opposite:] THE BIG KICK (Hal Roach, 1930). (The Museum
of Modern Art, New York City)

rather satisfied with himself as he shuts the door behind him.
The viewer would soon discover his reason for locking his
door from the inside.

Langdon looks just as he did in his classic Sennett
shorts. Although film historian William K. Everson has commented that Langdon was hurt by advancing age, the telltale
signs had not yet become apparent.

At the top of the stairs, Harry runs into the owner's
lovely daughter, with whom he is smitten. She exhorts him
to stop letting the other residents push him around. He
must stand up for himself! Moments later, the bully (Jim)
has tripped Harry on the stairs, sending him crashing to a
bad fall. Clearly, the Little Elf--the Shrimp--is the whip-
ping boy of the tenants, who make his humble life miserable
by their cruel practical jokes.

Even after running the gauntlet to the breakfast table
(suffering another pratfall and a kick in the pants along the
way), he grace no better. After the grace is said, Harry is
temporarily penned in by jutting elbows from both sides,
which keep him from lifting his arms to eat. Arms reaching
for food further frustrate his attempts to get to his plate. A
huge metal coffee pot is (inadvertently) pressed against his
face, burning one of his puffy cheeks. Before the meal is
over, Jim has shoved Harry's face into a huge bowl of berries.

Harry needs a miracle, and he gets it. A mad scien-
tist is conducting an experiment, for which he requires a human volunteer who is a proven coward. Harry is escorted
into the medical arena (before an audience) by a guard. He
will be the first one to test the doctor's serum, which has
been derived from a feisty bulldog. Within seconds, Harry
is jumping to his feet, throwing punches into the air. "I
can lick you, and you, and all of you!" he declares boldly.
"I can even lick Jim!"

With thoughts of revenge, Harry breaks free of the
scientists and soon finds himself on the front porch of the
house. There he kisses his girl (which he had never had
the guts to do before) and pushes Thelma out of his way.

Inside, the plucky Elf orders the lazy owner to work
and insists that his wife stop scrubbing the floors. When
Jim tries to intervene, he and Harry launch into a wild free-
for-all through the living and dining rooms. Dishes fly, and

Harry brandishes a wicked-looking fire poker.   "You see
what might happen--any time now?" Harry asks as he metes
out the punishment.   To cement his victory over the bully,
he ritualistically pushes Jim's face into a bowl of berries.
The gag has come full circle.

But the bulldog serum has one unforeseen side effect.
When Harry spots a cat jumping out the window, he follows
in hot pursuit, stopping only briefly before a telephone pole
to consider its possible uses.

THE SHRIMP demonstrates that the Roach staff made
considerable efforts to maintain the fundamentals of Langdon's
famous screen personality.   His helpless insecurity is evident from the beginning, and his triumph over his torment
is made possible (essentially) by forces outside himself.
Providence, once again, is his best friend.

Yet the gimmick of the film, the character transfor-
mation, provides surprisingly few moments of real mirth.
Harry's humor had always originated from his small, delicate mannerisms.   The feisty Harry of the second half of
THE SHRIMP showed a side of Langdon's behavior that is
outside his métier.

The "smaller" moments in the film are the best.
During the long (relatively wordless) routine at the breakfast
table, Harry is close to his old self as he reacts to a myriad
of major and minor irritations.   But the plot forces Harry to
be the butt of cruel comic violence.   That type of violence
was a trademark of Laurel and Hardy, and the Roach writers
were trying to adapt it for Langdon.

The comic reversal at the end of THE SHRIMP is
simply too ponderous.   That type of mechanical plotting was
an extension of certain gag motifs that Roach had perfected
with Stan and Ollie.   Hardy was going to experience pain due
to Stan's stupidity, that much was known far in advance.
When the damage is about to be inflicted, the audience has
seen disaster coming all along.   The laughs derive not only
from the pain inflicted, but from the absurdly ritualistic nature of the violence.   (This was especially true in their many
exercises in mutual abuse.)   When Roach extended the pre-
dictability of these gags to the structure of an entire two-
reeler, as he did with THE SHRIMP, the gag takes too long
to reach resolution.   The viewer can derive little pleasure
watching Harry give Jim his comeuppance, when he has seen

Langdon and his new bride, the former Mrs. Helen Walton,
<u>circa</u> 1929.   (Wayne Powers Collection)

it coming for several minutes.   Where is the humor in Harry
becoming a worse bully than Jim?

In one way, Langdon pulled through better than expected.   He was in no way intimidated by the transition to
sound.   He had spoken on the vaudeville stage without a
problem.   In a playful mood, Harry announced that his wedding to his second wife, Helen Walton, would be filmed with
sound for future reference.   In case of a quarrel, his wife's
vows to "love, honor and obey" could be replayed as a re-
minder.

Of all the giants of silent film comedy, Harry's voice
was the best suited to his character.   Chaplin spoke like a
genteel, Oxford-educated gentleman, which posed problems
if that voice was to issue from the lips of a tramp.   Lloyd's
voice was adequate, but seemed a trifle too thin and cultured.
Keaton's was low and gravelly, and could quickly become
monotonous.   Langdon's voice couldn't have been better.   He
had a high-pitched, slightly raspy inflection that perfectly
suited the Little Elf.   The only problem was that it got in
the way of his pantomime.

Buster Keaton had proposed that his talkies wouldn't
necessarily eschew long, basically silent sequences.   He
pointed out that people don't talk constantly, and that he
needn't speak unless it contributed importantly to the story
or the gag.   This approach would have been ideal for Langdon.   But the studios had just spent large sums building
soundproof sets and developing new equipment.   They wanted
their movies to talk, and for awhile films subordinated action
to conversation.   Courtroom dramas exemplified this trend
and enjoyed a brief vogue with pictures like THE BELLAMY
TRIAL, MADAME X and THE TRIAL OF MARY DUGAN.

There was never any doubt that Harry would talk in
his new films, and that his voice was not an obstacle in itself, but the writers seemed uncertain what the Elf would
say.   No comedian ever needed words less than Harry Langdon.

Talk destroyed the magical cloak of silence that had
imbued Harry's elfin character with a universal touch.   Silence had complemented his mental vagueness, allowing the
viewer extraordinary latitude to fill in the thoughts (or lack
of same) of that improbable creature.   Sound made Harry
literal, and the literal fact of a middle-aged man acting like

an infant could verge on the grotesque. Silence had allowed
his glacial thought processes to seem quaint; in these early
talkies, he became more an idiot than an elf.

The most overlooked aspect of the transition to sound
was the effect that the addition of sound had on the actual
screen image. Talkies were not simply silent films that
spoke. A synchronized sound track meant that the camera
had to crank at a standardized speed when filming the action.
Sequences that had been cranked faster to give added energy
to the proceedings were lost forever, unless the sound could
be dubbed in at a later date.

With the coming of sound speed (24 frames per second, as opposed to 16 to 18 frames per second in the silent
era), the movements and appearance of film comedians were
irretrievably altered. Instead of appearing nearly weightless,
sound speed added further realism to Harry's movements.
Not only did he talk, he looked different: more solid, less
agile. His footwork no longer seemed effortless, when the
viewer could hear his shoes scuffling on a sidewalk and his
clothes rustling. Langdon's former zip was missing. Even
if Harry had been in his prime in 1929, and could have af-
forded more time and care in adapting the Elf to talkies, a
successful transition would probably have remained elusive.
The obstacle was inherent in the very fabric of sound cinema.

Sound itself didn't kill Langdon the funnyman (as some
suppose), but it spelled doom for the Little Elf. Elves and
reality could not mix. Although the Elf's demise would not
be officially recorded for another five years, he really ended
his precarious existence in 1929 in Culver City.

*   *   *

What could have been the successful first step of his comeback developed into a tumultuous, demeaning experience for
Harry. Despite adequate production values, Langdon was not
happy with his treatment at the studio. Although nominally
a friend, Roach was wary of the former star. According to
Harry, Roach admonished him in an early meeting that he
would not put up with "that high handed stuff you pulled at
First National."[7] Langdon was on the defensive from the
start.

In truth, the films range from passable to awful.
Langdon found himself suffocated by slapstick plots that

wouldn't let him be. One of the central paradoxes of Langdon's career was that he achieved subtlety at Sennett, but
languished in uninspired farce at Roach. Even though he had
a keen understanding of film comedy, the producer failed to
understand that Harry's character best revealed itself in the
slower passages with broader physical action serving basically as a counterpoint.

When Langdon argued with his directors, Roach occasionally stepped in to complete the directing chores. He
observed that Harry would rehearse at a normal pace, then
slow down when the cameras were turning. He attributed
this to excessive ego on the part of the comedian. Harry's
friends, Roach claimed, had told him that he could stretch
out a scene longer than any other comic.

Time has shown that Hal Roach had a limited appreciation for Langdon's capabilities. Years later, when citing
the great screen clowns, he included Fatty Arbuckle but made
no mention of Langdon. Roach possessed a considerable
comedy ego of his own, and may have felt that if he could
not make Harry funny, then the fault lay with the comedian
himself. That the Roach/Langdon collaboration fell flat attests to the lack of chemistry between the styles of the two
men.

Of course, Harry Langdon was not without a sizeable
comedy ego. His contract gave him no script approval, but
he found it impossible to resist stating his opinions quite
forcefully. Again the gossip started: Langdon was difficult
to work with, uncooperative at every turn. No longer a big
star, he still acted like a big shot.

Harry Langdon walked off the friendliest lot in the industry in an angry, resentful temperament. Only three weeks
before, tempers had been smoothed over enough that he had
signed a second Roach contract for four feature films which
he would help write. But on March 31, 1930, the Hollywood
News reported: "Langdon Will Leave Roach." Ten months
in Culver City had been enough for Harry. Seven years
would pass before he would set foot on that lot again, under
far different circumstances.

NOTES

1. Photoplay, August 1928, p. 32.

2. Variety, March 20, 1929.
3. The New York Times, March 18, 1929.
4. Variety, March 20, 1929.
5. Photoplay, June 1929, p. 59.
6. Ibid., p. 102.
7. Photoplay, February 1932, p. 106.

Chapter Fourteen: COMEBACK

> "Having a jinx follow you is fun. At
> least there's never a dull moment."
> --Harry Langdon[1]

Once again, Harry made the headlines, but not because of his aborted contract with Roach. A new spate of notoriety centered on the comedian's love for Helen Walton, a bit player from one of his early films. A complicated legal action ensued when her husband, Thomas J. O'Brien, accused Harry of stealing his wife's affections.

Harry and Helen had begun seeing each other while both were still married; she had not legally separated from O'Brien. He contacted Langdon and threatened to sue for alienation of affections. The newspapers quickly picked up the story: "Funny Mr. Langdon's Not So Funny Promissory Love Notes" ... "Actor Denies Paying Balm to Wife's Ex-mate" ... "Film Star Denies He Stole Love of Engraver's Wife." Harry admitted that he had paid O'Brien $15,000 and signed promissory notes for an additional $11,500 as an out-of-court settlement. He had paid the "hush money" because he had been in the middle of some delicate contractual negotiations that might have been jeopardized by a lawsuit.

By 1930, Harry could not afford to pay the outstanding notes, so O'Brien took him to court. Langdon was vindicated, but the court ruled that O'Brien could keep the first $15,000. All that Harry had gained was expensive legal fees and public embarrassment.

Harry and former wife Helen were in and out of divorce
court during the late 1930's.   (Wayne Powers Collection)

Harry and Helen's stormy, short-lived union began on July 27, 1929. Although neither were alcoholics, both apparently drank heavily and quarreled incessantly. Most of their fights concerned money, for their marriage was plagued by financial instability. After the Langdons placed a downpayment for a house, they failed to make the payments. The owner threatened eviction and later charged them with petty theft for removing fixtures that belonged to the house. Harry was (again) exonerated in court, but the story was widely covered by the press.

If Helen Walton developed into something of a golddigger, Langdon must have deserved some of the blame. During their courtship, he had given her diamonds and furs, whetting her appetite for expensive things. Helen had originally declared that she would never ask Harry for alimony, whatever happened. She didn't believe in it. But by December 1931, when she sued for divorce, she had changed her mind. Now she demanded $1000 a week, a sum Langdon couldn't possibly pay.

Harry declared bankruptcy before the year was out. During his silent period, he had made nearly $1.5 million; now he listed debts of $60,000 (back taxes and miscellaneous debts) and assets valued at $700: a car worth $200, props and scenery for his vaudeville act worth $300, and $200 owed him by his attorney.

He appeared in only two films during this turbulent time. Ostensibly, he had left Roach to star in A SOLDIER'S PLAYTHING (Warner Bros., 1930), an unfortunate doughboy comedy with an oddly suggestive title. Although directed by the talented Michael Curtiz (CASABLANCA), the continuity is extremely episodic, leaving the impression that the released film was either severely truncated or never actually completed. The critics blasted it, and the public stayed away.

Universal's prohibition-era farce, SEE AMERICA THIRST (1930), fared little better. It teamed him with another alumnus of silent comedy, Slim Summerville. The New York Times wrote: "The audience ... appeared to be thoroughly amused at many of the incidents. It is, however, hardly a vehicle suited to Mr. Langdon's particular style of comedy."[2] The reviewer was reminded of "those old slapstick comedies" ... as if the silent era existed in the far distant past. Although deserving better, SEE AMERICA THIRST never found an audience and died at the box-office.

A SOLDIER'S PLAYTHING (Warner Bros., 1930).   (The Museum of Modern Art, New York City)

Harry Langdon's film career reached its nadir by the autumn of 1930. He didn't make a single film in 1931 and most of 1932. Frank Capra called Langdon "the most tragic figure I ever came across in show business." The proportions of that tragedy became apparent during the two years of enforced retirement from the screen. He had hit rock bottom.

Again, <u>Photoplay</u> helped advertise his wish to return to motion pictures. Harry's faith in his talent remained unshaken. "I can make good comedies ... if I'm not licked," he avowed.[3] This time, Langdon's appeal to the film producers fell on deaf ears. He had no choice but to return, once more, to the Keith circuit. He took his "After the Ball" act on the road, performing a grueling four shows a day for nearly a year.

Harry's live performances provided him with needed income, but nothing of the excitement of his month at the RKO Palace. Only comedians who couldn't find steady work in films resorted to the vaudeville stage in the 1930's. He probably realized, at this point, that he would never taste the heady elixir of major stardom again. As Harry gradually came to terms with this fact, some said his spirit was broken.

If so, he bounced back admirably when he learned that United Artists wanted him to provide important comic support in their new Jolson film. "It looks like I'm going to get a break at last," he told reporters. Harry was determined to be cooperative. Never again would his behavior on a soundstage be anything but acquiescent.

HALLELUJAH! I'M A BUM (1933) was envisioned as a unique form of musical. The music and lyrics were written by Rodgers and Hart, an auspicious portent, but the team failed to contribute a single memorable tune. S. N. Behrman's relatively normal dialogue segued into the musical sequences via recitative in rhyming couplets. Clearly experimental, the results were sometimes charming, but often stilted and forced.

The Depression-era story reflected the romantic opinion that the poor were wiser than the rich. It also espoused some left-wing politics. Harry played the role of Egghead, a litter collector in New York's Central Park. Jolson played the "mayor" of the hoboes who used Central Park as their headquarters. Langdon was fourth-billed, after Jolson, Frank Morgan, and Madge Evans.

SEE AMERICA THIRST (Universal, 1930), with Slim Summerville. (The Museum of Modern Art, New York City)

        The production was plagued with problems at the out-
set.   Director Harry D'Arrast was replaced by Lewis Milestone.   The budget soared to $1.25 million (then a large
sum for a film) when Frank Morgan replaced Roland Young,
and several major scenes had to be re-shot.   The title
changed almost daily, including HALLELUJAH! I'M A
TRAMP (the British title), NEW YORK, HAPPY GO LUCKY,
THE OPTIMIST, THE HEART OF NEW YORK, LIVING HIGH,
and LAZY BONES.   The final print was trimmed to a spare
eighty minutes, necessitating the deletion of several Langdon
bits.   Yet, amid all this turmoil, Harry never made trouble;
he was a model of professional aplomb.

        He worked deftly in the ensemble during some com-
plex musical numbers that required tight cues and split-
second timing.   Harry fits into the scheme of things quite
easily, even when he must play Jolson's attorney in a mock
trial.

The film affords him only one solo moment. He has gotten tipsy and the liquor bottle is stuck on his little finger. Every time he tries to bring his hand to his face, the bottle smacks him in the head. The accumulated booze and blows cause Harry to wave (his famous wave) as he tips over to the right in a final pratfall.

Despite some excellent reviews (<u>The New York Times</u> deemed it Jolson's best film), HALLELUJAH! I'M A BUM failed to click with the public. Jolson's initial superstardom in early talkies had waned (for his film acting was unbearably hammy) and the operetta-style rhyming recitative quickly palls. Still, Langdon was rated "effective" and "very ingratiating" and the film provided the first in a series of minor comebacks.

His next feature was a cameo appearance in a very special role. In Fox's MY WEAKNESS (1933), a musical comedy vehicle for British actress Lilian Harvey, Harry played Cupid. His interpretation was stylized, to be sure. His elderly version of the God of Love had a rather roguish, mature appeal. He functioned something like a one man

HALLELUJAH! I'M A BUM (United Artists, 1933), with Al Jolson. (Wayne Powers Collection)

Greek Chorus, commenting from a celestial vantage point on
the terrestrial action of the story.   This type of fantasy role
nicely suited Harry's talents, but he was never able to find
another role of this kind.

Langdon had difficulty landing parts in feature films.
His screen character was a product of the 1920's.   It had
been a time when innocence was widely felt to be beguiling
and appealing.   President Calvin Coolidge had been another
conspicuous symbol of the Bashful Age.   The changing tastes
that had contributed to Harry's downfall with THE CHASER
had solidified by the time the Depression took hold.

Harsh economic realities created a demand for comics
who were better able to cope with their cinematic problems
than the Elf, a perpetual study in ineptitude.   The comedy
sensations of the early 1930's were the Marx Brothers, W. C.
Fields, and Mae West.   Their humor crackled with cynicism
and sexual innuendo.   Their provocative amorality shocked
the stuffy bastions of tradition, to the delight of audiences
around the world.

Very soon, films like Howard Hawks' TWENTIETH
CENTURY (1934) ushered in the so-called "screwball comedies," where the focus was mainly on a verbal battle-of-the-
sexes.   The leading man and lady became the comedians, by
virtue of their wisecracks, insults, and erratic behavior.   A
supporting comedian was no longer required.   Ironically, the
other seminal film of this trend, IT HAPPENED ONE NIGHT
(1934), was directed by Frank Capra.

Langdon had to select among diminishing opportunities.
He accepted an offer that would return him to short comedy
again, a format that was now firmly linked with "B" film
production methods.   Certainly this was the case at Educational Pictures.   Founder Earle W. Hammons had given up
his original idea of making instructional pictures to enter the
more lucrative comedy market.   By the 1930's, it was clear
that Educational could amount to nothing, and its slogan, "The
Spice of the Program," was often the funniest joke in their
films.

Educational was the bargain basement of the short subject industry.   They made their name, such as it was, pre-
senting "the best of the old favorites, the brightest of the
new stars."   The implication was that anyone but a newcomer
or a has-been would steer clear of Educational.   A combination

THE BIG FLASH (Educational Films, 1932).   (The Museum
of Modern Art)

THE BIG FLASH (Educational Films, 1932), with Lita Chevret. (The Museum of Modern Art)

of a distribution deal with Fox and cut-rate budgets allowed the firm to realize a profit no matter how horrible the films might be.   Eighty percent of their product was sheer garbage. Yet, Educational had a useful place, for they provided work for talent that could (for any number of reasons) find no other showcase.   Both Buster Keaton and Mack Sennett eventually found their way to the Astoria, Long Island soundstages of Educational in the 1930's.

After paying the star's salary, very little was left for "minor" items like scripts and sets.   A short comedy might be budgeted as low as $20,000, with $5,000 going to the star. If the quality of the resultant film was hopelessly slipshod, the pay was good enough for the actors involved to swallow their pride.

In 1933, Harry made eight two-reelers for Educational's Mermaid Unit, beginning with THE BIG FLASH.   Most were

directed by Arvid E. Gillstrom. When these were completed,
he moved (with Gillstrom) to Paramount for five more shorts
which are virtually indistinguishable from the Educational
films. For the last time, Harry played the Little Elf (wearing his official costume, often augmented by white gloves and
a scarf) and was teamed once again with his old foil, Vernon
Dent (who received co-billing). [4] Harry Edwards directed
MARRIAGE HUMOR during the Paramount phase, adding to
the link with Harry's classic Sennett comedies.

In many ways, Langdon's Educational/Paramount series
was a successful attempt to rekindle the old slapstick style of
the Sennett days. Although they rely heavily on physical gags,
the films do not altogether neglect Harry's pantomimic ability.
Gillstrom was smart enough to let Langdon do what he did
best. The loose nature of the scripts added an air of spon-
taneity that the Roach series lacked.

They borrowed freely from Langdon's earlier successes,
a common practice. Perhaps the most effective reprise took
place in THE HITCHHIKER (1933), where Harry again has a
cold and seeks a remedy that turns out to be Limburger
cheese. The performance was mostly in pantomime. The
main changes were the setting (an airplane) and the actor who
played the irritated passenger (Vernon Dent).

Sadly, Harry was unable to resuscitate most of his
routines with as much flair. In KNIGHT DUTY (1933), one
of the poorest of the Educationals, the seduction of Little
Harry (again from THE STRONG MAN) is reduced to a quick
scene where a moll tries to retrieve a lost ruby (instead of
stolen money) from Harry's coat pocket. Rather than following the basic outlines of the original gag sequence (not a difficult task), the sequence throws away the character material
and is good for no more than one or two small laughs.

The single inventive sequence occurs in a silent vig-
nette near the opening, as Harry performs some fancy footwork on a sprinkler hose in an effort to recover his hat without getting wet. Langdon's balletic tightrope walking is cleverly punctuated by squirts of water each time his feet leave
the hose. The chief pleasure of viewing the Educational shorts
comes from the discovery of little gems like the sprinkler
routine.

The scripts, sets, and costumes are so poor that it
would be pointless to look for meanings in these crude yet

Harry and Vernon Dent repeating the "cold scene" from THE
STRONG MAN in THE HITCHHIKER (Educational Films, 1933).
(The Museum of Modern Art)

infectious comedies. With lowered expectations, however,
the viewer can find much to enjoy in the series. HOOKS
AND JABS (1933) seems to go nowhere until Harry finds himself in a boxing ring as a training partner of a neighborhood
pug. His babyish unawareness of the lethal nature of the
punches that come his way is Langdon at his best. So is
his fancy footwork when hit, and the misty expression that
comes into his eyes as the blows take their toll. Of course,
Harry (accidentally) knocks out the boxer.

THE STAGE HAND (1933) is arguably Langdon's best
Educational short, especially in terms of its concept and
story. Significantly, this comedy (the last of the first Educational eight) was written and directed by Langdon. He
plays the stage hand of an extremely amateurish theatrical
company in a small midwestern town.

The company is headed by a stuffy middle-aged matron named Mrs. Winters. The cast is completing rehearsals of an old-fashioned melodrama to raise money for a new fire engine. Having disrupted those rehearsals with his childish imitation of a doorbell, the Elf is lured into a secret room nearby by an older gentleman who speaks with an exaggerated German accent.

"SHHHH ..." the guy whispers, "come in ..." Harry enters the tiny room. "This is a shpeakeasy," the German explains. "I built the place myself. No one knows nothing about it, just myself ... unt Mrs. Vinters. Look, all private."

"Nice ..." Harry mumbles, checking out the place. "Private, huh?"

"Yah, yah ..." his friend mutters, pouring a drink. What follows is an elaborate drunk scene. Harry is repeatedly coaxed into drinking straight shots of vodka, even though he keeps trying to draw himself a beer from the keg. The two actors improvise the scene masterfully, descending quickly into idiocy, as the Elf becomes quite drunk ("Whooop--WHOOPEEE!") with the German gentleman shushing him. By the time Mrs. Winters finally finds them, Harry is totally bombed, collapsed in a heap on the floor, covered with beer foam.

As the performance is about to begin, Harry is preparing his sound effects equipment when the German (apparently an employee of the theater) approaches and asks: "You gonna ring the bell on the stage here? You got a union card?" Harry shakes his head. "Oh, well then you don't ring the bell here." The two scuffle (for the Elf has a strong sense of duty) and Harry falls onto the stage in full view of the audience.

He makes a hit with the local crowd with a spontaneous comic dance (similar to THE STRONG MAN). He manages to get some stage-frightened actors to perform a clever burlesque of small-town theater, and eventually demolishes part of the building while trying to guide a runaway fire engine on stage for the finale.

THE STAGE HAND has all of the usual Educational shortcomings, including a jumbled, confusing chase at the end. The slapdash nature of these productions becomes painfully

apparent when even a minimal amount of cinematic technique
is required. In front of a stationary camera, the comedian
could "punch up" pallid material, improvising and adding gags.
But the shoestring budget left him powerless to mount a con-
vincing action sequence.

Still, Langdon's original story is clever and entertaining. THE STAGE HAND is the closest in spirit to the Mack
Sennett comedies. After viewing the film, one can imagine
the Elf continuing as a viable screen clown into the sound
era, at least on a modest scale. Given a modicum of control, Langdon created nearly-exceptional comedy, even at
Educational. Unfortunately, he never received another screen
credit as director.

NOTES

1. Photoplay, February 1932, p. 106.
2. The New York Times, December 12, 1930.
3. Photoplay, February 1932, p. 40.
4. Dent co-wrote several of these films, with Dean Ward,
    including the entire Paramount series.

Chapter Fifteen: THE END OF THE ELF

When the president of Columbia Pictures, Harry Cohn, asked comedy director Jules White to organize a short subject department for the growing studio, White quickly assembled the most impressive array of comedy talent in the short comedy business, filling the gap left by Roach when he moved into features.

The new two-reeler production unit was envisioned as an important arm of Columbia, a studio that had only recently been turning out films that could compete with the "majors" like M-G-M and Warner Bros. Jules White inaugurated a series starring the Three Stooges that took off instantly; he soon enlisted Edgar Kennedy, Buster Keaton, Andy Clyde, and many others. Feeling that Harry had been plagued by undeserved bad luck, but could still hold his own as a comedian, White signed Langdon in 1934.

When the deal was closed, Harry granted an interview to the Los Angeles Examiner. His hard knocks during the early years of sound film had made him somewhat philosophical. He told the reporter,

> All this business of being a big shot--I've found it really doesn't mean much after all. It wasn't many years ago that my name was in lights emblazoned on billboards in huge letters. Certainly, it was pretty swell and all that. I can't deny that I enjoyed it. But Fate or whatever it is played tricks with me. I sat around relaxing and writing and sculpting for quite awhile. That became tiresome, so I decided to go back into pictures.

They're not feature length any more, but that's
nothing. And they've taken away the sloppy clothes
that were so much a part of my character and are
dressing me up like a fashion plate. That's not so
bad. I rather like it.

And last but not least, if I didn't have anything
else to be ridiculously happy about it wouldn't matter at all, for I'm going to be a father pretty soon!
That's enough to take care of any amount of unhap-
piness that might come along. [1]

On February 12, 1934, shortly before Langdon started
his first film for Columbia, he married for the third time.
His new bride was Mabel Georgena Sheldon.   On December
16 of that year, Harry, Jr. was born.   Harry declared,

I've seen all the Hollywood parties and night life
I want to see.   What I want now is a fireplace, a
wife and my police dog.   Contentment means much
more to me now than money.

For his new Langdon series, White wisely brought in
several of the comedian's old associates and friends: Arthur
Ripley, Harry Edwards, Alf Goulding, Vernon Dent, and Bud
Jamison.   Ripley directed the debut film, COUNSEL ON DE
FENCE (1934), originally announced as THE BARRISTER.
Edwards worked on the story.   Columbia put some money
into it, allowing for several spacious sets and well-populated
crowd scenes.

The story casts Harry as "Darrow Langdon," a bumbling barrister who has been retained to defend an alleged
poisoner, Antoinette "Toni" Drake.   Harry has many amusing
moments in the impressively mounted courtroom scene, where
he rises solemnly to address the jury, impulsively sticking
out a stiff arm to shake hands with them (a familiar Langdon
gesture), then gets his foot snared in a wire waste basket.
The climax comes when Harry swallows Exhibit A (the "poison") to prove that it is harmless.   When he learns that the
stuff is, indeed, quite deadly, he must first wait for the ver-
dict ("Not Guilty!") then extricate himself from the congratu-
latory mob before he can find a doctor to pump his stomach.

COUNSEL ON DE FENCE provides Langdon with many
gag opportunities, perhaps too many.   One of its flaws is
that it is too ambitious and tries to cram too much into its
short length.   Rather than develop a few good ideas, it jumps

from scene to scene haphazardly.   The editing is quite clumsy
at times.   A reprise of the dummy/policeman sitting on the
crate that contained his sweetheart, which proved to be one
of the most popular scenes in LONG PANTS, failed to successfully rework the routine.   Without the careful pacing,
structure, and camera angles of the original, the sequence
seems sloppy and underdeveloped.

Significantly, the film is Langdon's first two-reeler in
which he completely shed the persona of the Little Elf.   Gone
is his costume and with it, much of his childish manner.   He
grew a small moustache, which he wore in several other
Columbia shorts.   He was getting older, and his new bosses
felt it was time for Harry to move on.   The make-up could
no longer completely mask the signs of advancing age.   Not
that his basic mannerisms changed drastically.   He became
less the comic moron and more an absentminded, milquetoast
sort of fellow. [2]

Probably the best format Columbia developed for Harry
was the domestic comedy.   Basically, White up-dated the
main ingredients of SATURDAY AFTERNOON.   In the new
films, Harry was often supported by Ann Doran, an actress
who specialized in playing horrendously malicious wives. [3]
In essence, they played an exaggerated version of Blondie
and Dagwood, a series that was shooting on those same sound
stages.

In HIS BRIDAL SWEET (1935), Harry and Geneva
Mitchell are newlyweds whose honeymoon in a model house
is disrupted by all manner of "convenience" gadgets.   In I
DON'T REMEMBER (1935), Harry's lousy memory drives his
wife crazy.   In HIS MARRIAGE MIX-UP (1935), Harry lost
his wife-to-be and fell into the clutches of an axe murderess
in another situation inspired by LONG PANTS.

The first eight Columbia comedies were moderately
successful.   They were slickly photographed, included occasional location work, and featured very capable supporting
actors.   Often Vernon Dent stepped in to play Langdon's best
friend or adversary.

A DOGGONE MIX-UP (included here in the first group,
even though it was not made until 1938) ranks overall as the
best of the Columbia series.   Harry (using his own name for
his character) played a sucker who can't resist any bargain.
"I can't help it," he moans.   "There's some men that can't

resist drink, then there's some men that can't resist gam-
bling ... and I can't resist buying." His co-workers are
well aware of Harry's weakness. One manages to sell him
a dog collar. Only after making the purchase does he remember that he doesn't have a dog. After a salesman com-
pounds his dilemma by selling him dogfood and a doghouse,
Harry succumbs and buys a huge sheep dog named Herbert.

His wife (Doran) hates Herbert on sight. The first
thing the dog does is eat their dinner. When Harry tries to
put the dog in the backyard of their apartment building for
the night, Herbert tears down the landlady's laundry. Harry
ends up stumbling repeatedly into the huge metal garbage
cans, waking all the tenants. "Get rid of that dog or don't
come back!" his wife hisses, shoving them out onto the sidewalk.

"I hate to do this Herbert. Y'see, I'm not mad at
you ... but they are in there. So ... you gotta go. G'wan,
beat it - shooo!" Thinking his pet has taken the hint, Harry
prepares for bed. "--and take good care of Herbert," Harry
intones, kneeling for his prayers. "Please send him back to
me some time." Harry's prayers are quickly answered, as
the canine slips back into the house somehow and licks his
face.

In the morning, when his wife discovers that the dog
has returned, Harry asks: "Aw honey ... why don't you
give him another chance? He has such sweet and gentle
ways about him."

"GENTLE WAYS!!" she shrieks, as Herbert chases
their cat and tears down the drapes.

Kicked out of his apartment, Harry makes two more
purchases: a trailer home and a parcel of land. The lot is
located on the edge of a cliff, outside of town. This time,
Herbert's destructive binge takes on a more serious note.
He releases the trailer hitch and the vehicle slowly lumbers
toward the cliff.

"Harry, I think we're moving," his wife comments.
"Naw, it's probably just the wind shaking the trailer," he
replies. "Think nothing of it."

The trailer tips and dangles, stuck on the very edge
of the cliff. Trying to ascertain the trouble, Harry climbs

out a window and steps out onto ... nothing. "HERBERT!"
he screams. "HELP ME!"

Herbert finally does something right. With seemingly
super-canine strength, Herbert pulls the trailer (via a rope
attached to the hitch) back onto solid ground. He has saved
the day. "Thanks, pal, you saved my life!" Harry exclaims,
taking the rope from Herbert. He has forgotten that the dog
is much stronger than he is. The trailer goes over the cliff,
pulling Harry after it. As in TRAMP, TRAMP, TRAMP and
THE CHASER, the cliff turns out to be something more like
a 45-degree incline.

Fortunately, Ann (who was inside the trailer the whole
time) suffers nothing more serious than having her head stuck
in a bucket. After he frees her (accompanied by an amplified
"pop!" on the soundtrack), Harry swears: "I promise you
I'll never buy anything more as long as I live!" But his re-
solve fades when a fast-talking salesman arrives on the scene
of the accident offering "bargain" insurance. Enraged, his
wife chases him off into the distance, whacking him on the
posterior with a two-by-four.

A DOGGONE MIX-UP managed to generate some of
the old Langdon magic. Harry's devotion to the destructive
animal is both amusing and touching. His reluctant attempt
to get rid of Herbert achieves mild pathos. He had always
had a great affinity for animals. To this extent, the film
successfully conjures up touches from his best silent films.

Sadly, the Columbia series is a wildly uneven group
of films, sometimes descending to the level of the worst of
the Educationals. If the series had been able to build upward
from A DOGGONE MIX-UP, these talking shorts might have
developed into something memorable. That the following film,
SUE MY LAWYER (1938), is one of the worst of the series
demonstrates quite clearly that the comedian's potential remained largely untapped at Columbia. If Langdon deserved
the credit for the success of his self-directed Educational
short, THE STAGE HAND, then he must also shoulder much
of the responsibility for the failure of SUE MY LAWYER, for
he wrote the original story.

The film superficially resembles COUNSEL ON DE
FENCE. Harry again yearns for a career as an illustrious
legal wizard. Although he lacks a law degree, he persistently
pesters District Attorney O. T. Hill (Bud Jamison) for a job.

Lobby card for SUE MY LAWYER (Columbia, 1938). (Michael Copner Collection)

He offers to help Hill prosecute the Red Burton murder case. Burton's sister Anita (Ann Doran) overhears Harry's empty boast that he has inside information that will convict the killer. In the parlor of her boarding house, Anita tries to lure Harry upstairs (into an ambush by her confederate) by promising him a kiss--if he will accompany her to her room. When Harry resists, she pretends to faint, thus forcing him to carry her up the stairs. (This sequence is a deliberate imitation of THE STRONG MAN.)

Alone in her room for a moment, Harry stumbles across the missing evidence (a pair of pants) but conceals the evidence when Anita Burton retains him as her lawyer. In court, Langdon inadvertently reveals that the D.A. can't convict Burton without the evidence--which he has in his possession. When Harry produces the pants to prove his point, a melee ensues, ending with the D.A. congratulating Harry on breaking the case.

Although it is perhaps unfair to expect too much consistency of character and motivation in a short film of this
kind, one can make very little sense out of Harry's behavior
here. He is certainly not motivated by any desire to see
justice done, for he tries to defend a man he knows to be a
brutal murderer (while suppressing evidence). If his judg-
ment is being influenced by affection for Anita (a passable
excuse), the point is not clearly made in the film. If not,
he is a very dangerous man indeed. In his classic films,
the Elf might very well attempt to defend (or befriend) a
killer--but would certainly run for cover once he learned the
truth. In SUE MY LAWYER, his character has no moral
consistency.

The pace was a problem for Harry. In Film Fan
Monthly, Jules White recalled: "I had a theory and it paid
off: make 'em move so fast, if they're not funny, no one
will have time to realize it or get bored. I didn't try to
be artistic, I just wanted audiences to laugh. They did."[4]

Frank Capra, now an Oscar-winning, prestigious director at Columbia, happened to peek at Langdon during the
shooting of SUE MY LAWYER. Harry was rehearsing the
scene where he carries Ann Doran up the stairs. According
to Capra, the director (White) was exhorting the comedian to
pick up the pace.

"I could have cried," Capra wrote. "That great,
great artist--whose art was the very essence of slow, slow
pantomime--was being hollered at to 'go faster!'"[5]

A comparison of the stairway sequence in SUE MY
LAWYER with the original in THE STRONG MAN demonstrates
how much film comedy depends on the director. With Langdon, camera angles took on paramount importance. Harry
Edwards and cameraman William Williams had learned in
their earliest Langdon films for Sennett that Harry's face and
body had to be carefully photographed to the best advantage.
Without a director with sensitivity to these subtler points,
the comedian could (and often did) come off as quite ordinary.

When Harry picks up Gertrude Astor in the silent film,
and begins mounting the stairs, the camera is set at a distance, looking straight at the stairs. Not only can the viewer
see Langdon's full figure, but much of the apartment building
lobby is visible. As a result, the momentousness of his task
is emphasized. Aware of Harry's persistent ineptitude, the

audience asks the question: "How will he ever make it?"
When he sits down and begins moving backward up the stairs
on his tail, the audience is charmed by the neatness of the
simple solution imposed on Harry by the forces of gravity.

In the re-make, the camera cannot look directly onto
the stairs, since the stairway is flush with one wall. Most
of the scene must be photographed from a three-quarters
angle in a medium-shot. One sees much of Harry's struggle, but none of the context so crucial to the comic effect
achieved by the first version. The camera angle does not
allow for the best use of Langdon's moon-shaped face, and
the pacing is too fast.

As in the original, Harry and the girl continue up a
janitor's ladder. The flip over the top and fall to the ground
are accomplished quite well. But after that, the two simply
get up and go about their business. Harry is given no chance
to add the hilarious embellishments of the original: the rubbery knees, his dazed expression--in short, his reaction to
the event. In SUE MY LAWYER, the fall itself is the conclusion. Without showing the shock waves on Harry's con-
sciousness, it is just one more brutal slapstick gag.

Though Langdon's ability could not fail to come across,
his special qualities became submerged in the Columbia series.
Instead of the absurd eccentricity he had achieved in his classic films, at Columbia he was only sporadically funny. His
initial originality gave way to a more generalized "goof" characterization. He worked as hard as ever, but the material
and other limitations of the series fought him at every turn.

Anticipating the coming of sound, Chaplin had worried
that if he talked, he would become too much like other comedians. To a large extent, this was the fate that befell Harry
Langdon.

NOTES

1. Los Angeles Examiner, September 14, 1934.
2. Occasionally, he would still don a hat that resembled his
    old one, and added a scarf (like the Educationals) in
    COLD TURKEY (1940).
3. Doran played a meatier version of this character in REBEL
    WITHOUT A CAUSE (1955), cast as James Dean's mother.
4. Film Fan Monthly, February 1969, p. 21.
5. The Name Above the Title, p. 72.

In 1935, Harry received an offer that excited him: the Victor Moore part in the musical comedy Anything Goes. The attractive aspect was that the production was to take place in Australia. The trip appealed to his wanderlust. He and Mabel would make an around-the-world adventure out of it. His contract with Columbia didn't include stage appearances, and after obtaining the blessings of Jules White, the Langdons caught a steamer down under. After fulfilling his obligation with the play, they would stop in England for a protracted visit. Mabel had relatives there.

The play was already a proven hit, so Harry had nothing to worry about on that score. He spent his afternoons drawing daily cartoons for the Sydney Times. He also wrote a series of articles on Hollywood for a Melbourne paper. He enjoyed being a "big fish" again, even if the size of the pond was small. Australia in the 1930's was definitely off the beaten track.

Upon their arrival in England, Harry and Mabel were experiencing a period of temporary insolvency. Expenses had been higher than expected. Langdon landed a cameo role in a Biltmore picture starring Ben Lyon, Lupe Velez, and Wallace Ford. MAD ABOUT MONEY (1937)[1] was a low-budget musical of dubious appeal, with lots of snappy dialogue, some clumsy dancing, and too many men and women in formal evening attire.

Langdon's part is obviously tacked on at the last minute. He essayed the role of theatrical "angel" (backer) Otto Schultz. Perhaps Harry's dimwitted antics were intended as

177

a comment on the now-threatening Aryan Race. His participation was limited to a turn near the opening (trying to sneak
past a busy producer's secretary) and some singing in a big
musical number toward the end.

The latter sequence is the most imaginative (and un-
believably corny) number in the film. As Otto gets drunk,
he sinks down to the table and falls asleep. In his dreams,
the movie's cast find themselves shooting through space in a
rocket ship. In outer space, they sing and dance on the
stars. MAD ABOUT MONEY did nothing for Harry's reputation, but it did alleviate his financial crisis.

Throughout the 1930's, Langdon had many ideas for
projects that never materialized. The trade papers announced
a dozen films that were definitely "set"--but which were never
made. During the production of SEE AMERICA THIRST, Universal hailed the start of a Langdon-Summerville series.
When the film did less than great business, future films were
scrapped.

One of the most interesting projects was Harry's idea
for a "Hollywood" nightclub in London. He designed an inti-
mate restaurant on a modest scale, with a small stage and
boxes along the walls. He would design bas-relief plaques
for the walls, in the likenesses of visiting celebrities. An
investor was even found, but at the last minute Langdon
changed his mind. Possibly the imminence of another World
War cast a pall over the project.

By the time Harry and Mabel returned to Los Angeles,
he had been off the screen (with the exception of MAD ABOUT
MONEY which received a scattered release in America) for
nearly two years. Although Harry always had plenty of projects to keep him busy, films had always provided most of
his income. It was time to pick up the pieces of his motion
picture career, and see if anything could be made of it.

Langdon's friendship with Stan Laurel probably dates
back to his disastrous first stint with Roach in 1929. Stan
had been a big fan of Harry's, and was not one to judge the
comedian too harshly when he fell on hard times. Stan let
Harry know that he would always consider him one of the
greats; he hung an autographed picture of the Elf in a prominent place in his study.

Harry and Oliver Hardy ("Babe" to his friends) shared

Langdon returned to the stage in the middle 1930's.   (Michael
Copner Collection)

several leisure interests in common. Both had a passion
for golf. Certainly, when the day's filming was completed
and Babe drove to the nearest golf course to play a few holes
with some pals, Langdon was often included in the group.
The Langdons and Hardys saw a lot of each other in other
settings. Several photographs show them together in restaurants or around a piano in song.

Laurel did not enjoy socializing; he seemed too high
strung to relax. He spent most of his spare time at the
studio. In truth, he was the creative force behind Laurel
and Hardy. He became deeply involved in the writing, directing, and editing of their comedies. After months of feuding with Roach the year before, he had set up "Stan Laurel
Productions" and Roach had agreed to give him full control
of their films.

Although the lines of communication between Laurel
and Roach were breaking down by the time Harry came to
Stan in 1937, Laurel promised Langdon a writing job on the
next film. Thus, when BLOCKHEADS was announced in the
summer of 1938, Harry became a gag-writer, and began
what was to be the most felicitous, fascinating chapter of
his sound film career.

The arrangement was beneficial to both parties. Langdon's thirty-five years as a comedian made him a gold mine
of funny ideas. His experience on the vaudeville stage probably cemented his relationship with Stan. Besides, their
comedy styles had undeniable similarities.

Both played child/men who possessed hardly a half a
brain, and didn't have the wits to pretend they had more.
Stan shared Harry's ability to totally immerse himself in
moronic behavior, while seeming to have his head in the
clouds. Both conveyed a kind of quiet whimsy that was essentially a quality of a silent clown. Even their bodies had
the same pear shape, since Stan's normally slender waistline
had grown to nearly rival Hardy's by this time.

Not that there weren't differences. Stan was less ex-
citable than Little Harry, who would scamper around uncon-
trolled at the slightest provocation. Laurel tended to remain
planted in one spot, perhaps leaning at a slight angle, while
his mind shifted over the latest occurrence. Laurel sustained
far more physical abuse (mostly from Ollie) than Harry was

ever to suffer at the hands of others.   Yet, Stan recognized
their overlapping qualities.   He may have felt glad to have
a graduate of the slapstick school at his side, when knockabout comedy (the form that Laurel and Hardy harkened from)
was suffering from hard times.   The advent of screwball
comedy had hurt Langdon earlier, because he was more vul-
nerable.   Now, the sophisticated comedies (generally featuring women like Carole Lombard and Irene Dunne) were putting
the squeeze on Stan and Ollie.

The opening sequence of BLOCKHEADS (1938) is virtually lifted from the opening scenes of Langdon's doughboy
silent for Sennett, SOLDIER MAN.   The World War is over
for everyone but Stanley.   Twenty years after the Armistice,
he still walks his guard watch, having worn down a whole
new trench in the process.   A mountain of empty bean cans
attests to the length of his vigil.

Not only did the film repeat the Langdon episode, it
re-cycled several Laurel and Hardy routines too.   Stan had
never been loathe to repeat himself, so long as he could
come up with a fresh variation to avoid sheer duplication.
No one seemed to care.   BLOCKHEADS (which had been announced as the team's last film together) received glowing
reviews.   The public still loved them.   It was Harry Langdon's lot to share in their reflected glory.

The feuding began again between Laurel and Roach.
Stan always threatened to go elsewhere and produce his own
comedies, but unfortunately for his negotiating position, Hardy
could not go with him.   Laurel and Hardy had never formalized their partnership as a legal entity.

Roach found it to his advantage to keep the two comedians under separate contracts, with Stan's expiring a year
before Babe's.   (This was not begun intentionally, since they
were put under contract before they became a team.)   Knowing that Stan would be eager to keep working, Roach could
use that lever to get a better deal.   Finally, with Stan again
demanding more money, Roach's patience wore thin, and he
fired Laurel.

Hardy remained under contract, and Roach had no intention of letting a good box-office draw sit idle.   Roach puz-
zled over the problem of finding a suitable vehicle for the
rotund comedian.   One idea paired him with Patsy Kelley in
a "Hardy Family" domestic series; it never got off the ground.

Although Hardy was primarily an actor (rather than a comic), and could have easily adapted to a number of different roles, Roach kept thinking of him as part of a team.

The writers had come up with a comedy first called IT'S SPRING AGAIN for Hardy. There was another smaller role, which Roach felt should be played by a comedian. For once, luck was on Harry's side. He had just played a cameo in the latest Roach release, THERE GOES MY HEART, which starred Fredric March and Virginia Bruce. Langdon appeared only briefly at the end as the Minister.

Going through Roach's mind was the reaction at a sneak preview when Langdon made his entrance. Murmurs of recognition and approving giggles convinced Roach that audiences still remembered Harry. Perhaps, Roach thought, there was still money to be made from the Langdon name.

He summoned Harry and broached his idea. Would Harry be willing to co-star with Oliver Hardy in IT'S SPRING AGAIN? It wouldn't be a true team-up at first, but they would share some scenes together. If audience response was satisfactory, follow-up films would be made. Besides, it would be a great opportunity for Harry. If Langdon needed any further persuasion, he was under contract.

He wanted to do the film, but Harry did not want to be used by Roach to hurt Stan. He contacted Laurel and told him of the offer. Laurel understood that Langdon couldn't afford to pass up the deal, and assured him there would be no hard feelings. The film, soon to be re-titled ZENOBIA, would be made with or without Harry. Stan encouraged him to take advantage of the break. Both comedians knew that the arrangement could only be temporary. Harry wanted Laurel and Hardy back together as much as did Stan.

The Roach publicity staff announced the new Langdon and Hardy team to the trade papers and columnists. Although touted mostly for publicity purposes, the story was newsworthy and evoked considerable curiosity. Persistent rumors for years had reported that Stan and Babe fought constantly. Although completely false, the new team-up seemed to lend credence to the gossip.

[Opposite:] Harry (center) relaxes with Stan Laurel (left) and Oliver Hardy (right). (Michael Copner Collection)

Langdon remained wary. After a decade of broken deals, missed opportunities, bankruptcy and damaging headlines, the public eye was not something he comfortably sought. Still, he had hope. The possibility of a minor comeback could not have completely faded from his mind. Langdon was guardedly optimistic about the new film. Perhaps it would open some doors.

Teaming Babe and Harry presented intriguing possibilities. Although Harry might always be perceived as a substitute for Stanley, he could have been a brilliant substitute. He had spent his whole career perfecting the kind of comic imbecility that would drive Ollie crazy. Adjustments would have been required. They could not both react. Like Stanley, Harry would have needed to play a more assertive, if no more intelligent, character. Babe might be given more to do. A pleasing chemistry could have developed, not unlike that symbiotic relationship Harry had shared with Vernon Dent. ZENOBIA was designed to test the water.

ZENOBIA (1939)[2] is a pleasant farce set in Mississippi in 1870. All of its characters are drawn in a simple, broad manner. The proceedings are all far more civilized than a Laurel and Hardy production. The inevitability of violent catastrophe is considerably subdued. The entertainment values lie mainly in the breezy dialogue and charming cast.

Oliver Hardy, as Dr. Emery Tibbitt, is a model of Southern gentility and impeccable manners. Billie Burke, as his scatter-brained wife, Bessie, cheerily spouts malapropisms and chirps about the house: "To work! To work!" Stepin Fetchit played their slow-witted servant Zero, pushing vocal abstraction to the brink of incomprehensibility. A nice surprise is Hattie McDaniel in a bit part as the robust family cook. She adds zest to the rather airy events that occupy the Tibbitt household.

Langdon doesn't appear for nearly fifteen minutes. First, the love story between Tibbitt's daughter Mary and the son of society snob Mrs. Carter (Alice Brady) must be established. The viewer learns that Tibbitt's medical practice is in jeopardy. He has alienated his rich patients by refusing to coddle their imagined illnesses, and is nearly broke from helping the sick, even when they can't pay his bill. Mrs. Carter has no intention of letting her son marry into Tibbitt's eccentric family.

Professor J. Thorndyke McCrackle (Langdon) becomes
involved in their lives in the unlikeliest way. He travels
with a small-time carnival (or is it a traveling medicine
show?) using his trained elephant Zenobia to draw the crowds.
He hawks his snake oil: "... a remedy that I've brought to
you at the risk of life and limb through the teaming jungles
of Borneo and across the burning sands of the Sahara!"

McCrackle pauses, dry-mouthed, for a sip of his
"tonic"--a concoction, he claims, "that will make you as
strong as an elephant!" The crowd applauds as Zenobia prepares to perform a trick. Suddenly, she sinks to the ground,
a victim of some mysterious illness. The Professor is
frightened, and it is clear that he has considerable sympathy
for the animal. He frantically summons Dr. Tibbitt.

Their first scene together centers around a breakdown
in communication. Tibbitt thinks McCrackle's wife is sick.
He is stunned when he is informed that "she" is 104 years
old, and weighs over 6,000 pounds. Babe does a massive
double-take.

When Tibbitt does discover the truth, he is at first
reluctant to help. He can't be seen treating an elephant.
McCrackle insists, and Tibbitt quickly spots what he thinks
is the problem: a knot in Zenobia's tail. She revives as
soon as the minor damage is undone. In a further examination scene, they divide Zenobia up into "zones" (head, side,
feet) and give her a complete physical.

What Tibbitt doesn't expect, or need, is for Zenobia
to fall madly in love with him. Just when his every action
must be socially correct (to try to please Mrs. Carter), the
elephant follows him relentlessly, leaving a trail of carnage
and hysteria in her wake.

Zenobia has scant regard for social customs, and
doesn't hesitate for a moment to crash Mrs. Carter's elaborate society party to be near the Doctor. When it becomes
obvious that the animal is smitten with Tibbitt, the town
treats him like a social pariah. Bessie is so worked up,
she won't allow him in the house. The wedding is, of course,
called off.

What's worse, McCrackle sues Tibbitt for alienation
of affections. It is difficult to believe that the ensuing court-

ZENOBIA (Hal Roach/United Artists, 1939), with Oliver
Hardy.   (Wayne Powers Collection)

room scenes were not (even tangentially) intended as a parody
of the legal problems that plagued Langdon in earlier years.

     The Professor practices his testimony before Mrs.
Carter and her attorney. "Well, in the first place, Zenobia
and I...." He learns it so well, he can't wait to recite it.
In court, he jumps up at the first opportunity and launches
into it. When the judge finally allows him on the witness
stand, McCrackle's testimony abruptly segues into his canned
salespitch. Very soon, he is coaxing everyone to "step right
up" and hear about his miraculous nerve tonic. The case is
thrown out of court, when the judge realizes that there is no
penalty for stealing an elephant's love.

     Roach gave the final scene to Harry. McCrackle walks
away from the crowds who see him off. He strides down a
country lane, wearing his top hat and carnival coat. His be-
loved Zenobia is at his side. The group is joined by a third

member: Zenobia's baby, for her problem all along had been
an undetected pregnancy.

As the music swells on the soundtrack, Harry turns
and waves to the wedding party (and the movie audience).
He seemed to be saying: "Goodbye for now, but don't worry
--I'll be back!" The sentimental ending was touching, especially for anyone who fondly remembered Harry, and all the
wonderful moments he had contributed to screen comedy in
the past.

                            *   *   *

The impressive production values are the best thing about
ZENOBIA. The declining popularity and profits in short
comedies caused Hal Roach to exclusively turn to feature
film production. He wanted to compete with the top studios,
and did (for a time) with films like TOPPER, OF MICE AND
MEN, and ONE MILLION B.C. ZENOBIA benefitted from
the new polished "Roach look." It ranks well above the "B"
picture level. After enduring excrutiatingly cheap production
at Educational and other studios, Harry was pleased to be in
a film where the technical or budgetary shortcomings didn't
sabotage his performance.

Even though they had two of the greatest American
comedians at their disposal, the writers gave the best material to the rest of the cast. The gag sequences with Langdon and Hardy lack pacing and snap, perhaps because they
had to be constructed around the behavior of a live elephant.
The animal "sits" on Tibbitt, lifts him in her trunk and carries him on her back--stunts, not gags. The events are
light-hearted and entertaining, but not overly funny.

McCrackle was not the usual type of casting for Langdon. The brash carnival huckster had already become W. C.
Fields' most memorable persona. The Professor is close to
the villain of the piece (after Mrs. Carter). Harry handled
the part with professional bravado, imbuing McCrackle with
a sympathetic, believable character. Langdon was more ver-
satile than ever expected.

Of the several features in which Harry lent his support, ZENOBIA is the best. It certainly ranks as the most
significant sound picture he ever made. The reviews tended
to greet his "return" in a positive light. The New York
Times wrote: "Harry Langdon's pale and beautifully blank

countenance has probably already excited the artistic jealousy
of Mr. Laurel."[3]

The cancellation of the follow-up to ZENOBIA came
as a major blow to Langdon. He entertained no illusions
about the longevity of a Langdon and Hardy partnership, but
he had eagerly anticipated the second film, since it had been
envisioned as a genuine team comedy. Before filming began
on ZENOBIA, Bert Kalmar and Harry Ruby were writing the
next one.

A mediocre box-office showing caused the second picture to be dropped, and with it, Langdon's last real chance
to make a big impression. He had counted on the exposure
with Hardy to consolidate his return to the screen. Instead,
the mixed reception to ZENOBIA effectively ended Harry's
last minute end-run.

Nevertheless, Harry and Stan became closer than ever.
Langdon spent many evenings with the comic in his country
home, Ft. Laurel. Although Stan could never manage women,
to his extreme detriment, he was fiercely loyal to his co-
workers and male friends. Whenever he made plans, and he
made many during those idle months, it was understood that
Harry would have a place in them.

Langdon was undoubtedly becoming aware of certain
parallels between their careers. Almost unthinkably, Laurel's
standing in the industry was in serious jeopardy. His love
affairs had too often been in the headlines, and word was out
that he was "difficult to work with," the ultimate Hollywood
damnation.

All this was painfully familiar to Harry. He must
have experienced an unpleasant sensation of déjà vu. He
evinced enthusiasm for Laurel's plans for independent comedies
of a Chaplinesque stature. For himself, Harry no longer
dreamed that big. After the disappointment with ZENOBIA,
Langdon seemed satisfied to take whatever came his way.

Stan made sure Harry had a writing job on the next
Laurel and Hardy feature, FLYING DEUCES (1939). Now
that Hardy was free, they accepted a production offer from
Boris Morros for RKO release. Harry followed the team
back to Roach for A CHUMP AT OXFORD (1940) and SAPS
AT SEA (1940). On the latter film, a start date arrived before the script was begun, so Stan, Harry, and the other

writers improvised one day at a time. Whatever standing
sets on the lot were available were pressed into service.
Despite the chaotic genesis of SAPS AT SEA, it stands as
the last of the great Laurel and Hardy features.

Stan and Ollie never worked for Hal Roach again.
The team was forced to move to a B-film unit at Twentieth
Century-Fox. The subsequent Fox (and M-G-M) comedies
devastated the team and their fans. They were looking old
and tired, their comedy seemed dated, and other comedians
(notably Abbott and Costello) had superseded them. Worst
of all, the writing was atrocious. Laurel could not invite
Langdon aboard when he was not allowed to work on the
scripts himself.

Roach found more work for Langdon. Harry appeared
in a "streamliner" (a series of Roach comedies with forty-
five- to fifty-minute running times) called ALL-AMERICAN
CO-ED (1941) in the smallish part of a press agent who spon-
sors a college beauty contest. He was hired as a writer for
ROAD SHOW (1941). But when Roach (at age 48) was inexplicably drafted into the Army the following year, the studio
was commandeered by the Pentagon for the duration, and
Langdon was obliged to find employment elsewhere.

NOTES

1. Distributed in the U.S. as HE LOVED AN ACTRESS by
   Grand National.
2. Known as ELEPHANTS NEVER FORGET in Britain.
3. The New York Times, May 15, 1939.

As work tapered off at Roach, Langdon's lagging Columbia series (there had only been two released films since 1935) began to pick up. The new cycle started with COLD TURKEY in 1940, but didn't really get going until WHAT MAKES LIZZY DIZZY? in 1942. In all, Harry made thirteen more films for Jules White. The new films were not much different in spirit or production values than earlier efforts like COUNSEL ON DE FENCE and HIS MARRIAGE MIX-UP.

Perhaps the most noticeable difference is in Langdon's appearance. No amount of make-up could successfully camouflage the effects of advancing age. Even in soft focus, the lines under his eyes and the sagging skin beneath his chin became apparent. The delicate, baby-faced illusion had been successfully maintained well into the sound era. Even with the comedian nearly fifty years old, he looked as convincingly youthful as ever in THE STAGE HAND (1933). As long as that famous face had to be retained, Harry succeeded in defying the passage of time and its effects. That day could not be postponed forever, but the decision was taken out of Langdon's hands when he signed with Columbia. Dropping the trademark costume meant more than abandoning his funny hat and jacket with the eight big buttons. It meant removing the veil from one of the most intriguing, eccentric illusions in the history of the cinema, and revealing the face behind the face. That face belonged to a man well into middle-age. By 1942, Harry was approaching sixty years old, and Columbia did not really attempt to hide that fact.

The ravages of time are particularly disturbing on

190

Langdon in these later films. Harry never strayed far from portraying an extremely dimwitted, scatterbrained person: essentially, a child. His movements, his posture, his gestures all conveyed the same infantilism he had projected at Sennett. Only the scripts--and his face--let the audience know that Langdon was really just a particularly silly adult.

His body could no longer sustain even the fairly mild abuse that it had in the past. Although never an acrobatic comedian like Buster Keaton, who did all save a few of his own stunts, Harry had been able to perform a credible pratfall at just the right moment. His backward fall out the open window (after kissing Natalie) in ALL NIGHT LONG is the best example. Yet, a close examination of even the earliest films reveals that Langdon and company depended quite heavily on stunt men all along. One of the worst abuses in the silent features is the bicycle ride around Bebe Blair's car in LONG PANTS. Some of the fancy work, in relative close-up, does belong to Langdon, but the cover shots substitute doubles. Those flashy stunts, most of which Harry did not perform, elicited a strong audience response. Presumably, the comedian on his own could not have scored as well with the same premise.

By the time he reached Columbia, Langdon's increasingly frail body could no longer sustain more than a mild pratfall. Yet the scripts, which often took their cue from SUE MY LAWYER, thrust him into all manner of violent situations. Often, the stunt work was all too obvious. For some reason, the writers included endless clunks on the head, smashes into doors, and falls from high places; it was as if they were trying to make a no-talent comedian funny. Perhaps that is what they thought. Harry could not only not sustain the physical punishment, he wasn't funny in that context.

Harry was again working with friends. Harry Edwards directed six of the new Columbias. Ann Doran returned to portray her patented harridan role in COLD TURKEY, which was a partial re-make of A DOGGONE MIX-UP. This time, Harry won a live turkey in the office Christmas raffle, and has to cope with the bird and a freshly painted kitchen floor. When chasing the bird around his apartment house with an axe (he had considerably less sympathy for the animal this time), Langdon is mistaken for a maniac. Of course, when Harry hears that a maniac is loose, he is scared out of his wits.

TO HEIR IS HUMAN (Columbia, 1944).   (Wayne Powers
Collection)

Bud Jamison, Harry's co-star in HIS FIRST FLAME
and THE CHASER, supported Langdon in A BLITZ ON THE
FRITZ (1943) and others. In these new films, Jamison's
portly figure was almost interchangeable with that of Vernon
Dent. Dent stayed with Langdon, playing his best friend or
adversary (sometimes no more than a brief cameo), and
therefore ranks as Harry's most frequent supporting actor.
Dent had found a comfortable niche in the Columbia short
subjects department, appearing in roughly half of the Stooges
films until 1956.

The later Columbias had one essential difference from
earlier Langdon two-reelers: Harry found himself in a supporting capacity. Until then, he had always been the star of
his short comedies. Now Columbia used him to build up per-
sonalities like Una Merkel, Elsie Ames, and Monty Collins.
The last four comedies in the series (beginning with DEFEC-
TIVE DETECTIVES, 1944) billed Langdon under El Brendel,
a Swedish dialect comic. Brendel had started in vaudeville,
and appeared sporadically in films during the 1930's. In the
1940's, Brendel was enjoying something of a vogue in radio
and found himself paired with Langdon.

The studio's usage of Harry's face in the advertising
indicates that they continued to feel that Langdon was a recognizable commodity that might sell more than a few tickets.
His roles in the films themselves were generally the largest.
He was grateful for the work.

Roles in feature-length films were harder for Langdon
to secure. After being trapped for so many years in B-grade
films, none of the major studios would touch him. During
the 1930's, he was occasionally given a part in a marginally
high-quality feature, often because a fantasy element was not
totally out of place in many films of that era. With the coming of World War II, fantasy was moved into the most realistic of contexts. Harry would no longer fit in.

Unable to fire up interest in the likes of M-G-M,
Paramount, Fox, or Universal, Harry turned to minor studios,
sometimes called "Gower Gulch," the "B-hive," or more com-
monly, "Poverty Row." After years of rubbing shoulders in
the lower echelons, Langdon had made many connections in
the fast-film outfits like Monogram and Republic, where his
name still meant something. Unfortunately, Langdon's first
official "B" film was made at a studio whose production values
were so wretched, they made Republic look like M-G-M.

MISBEHAVING HUSBANDS (PRC, 1940).   (Michael Copner
Collection)

Harry began working at the most poverty-stricken studio of
them all: Producers Releasing Corporation (PRC).

    It is difficult to convey in words the cheap look of
the average PRC film. The music consisted mainly of a
limited selection of scratchy library records. The sound
was often garbled and muddy, probably because no one bothered to check the recording levels. The film stock was the
least expensive (hence the grainiest) available. The sets
were seemingly constructed of cardboard and papier-mâché.

    There was very little to belie the grind-house appear-
ance of the PRC product. As was usual at a bottom-of-the-
barrel outfit, the studio attracted exclusively talent on the
way up, down, or in limbo. Some of the actors who graced
PRC films were Alan Ladd, Bela Lugosi, Forest Tucker,

Buster Crabbe, and Carl "Alfalfa" Switzer.   The supporting
actors were the worst, often no better than bad high school
dramatists.

Founded by Ben Judell in 1939, PRC took over the
facilities of Grand National (a defunct B-film studio that had
distributed Langdon's HE LOVED AN ACTRESS) and proceeded
to churn out endless ultra-low budget programmers along the
usual lines: westerns, mysteries, war stories, comedies.
Amazingly, PRC displayed a good deal of staying power,
something akin to crabgrass. In a field where the "lifespan"
of a studio averaged anywhere from one to three years, PRC
survived for seven. They did it through a combination of
canny promotion and sheer tenaciousness.

Against all odds, PRC managed to turn out a few films
of enduring interest. BEASTS OF BERLIN (1939) stands as
one of the first all-out anti-Nazi films, generating a lot of
controversy and a healthy box-office return. Their horror
films were occasionally interesting: THE DEVIL BAT, THE
DEVIL BAT'S DAUGHTER, DEAD MEN WALK, and STRAN-
GLER OF THE SWAMP (with Charles Middleton).

Not everyone ended up at PRC strictly out of desperation. Director Edgar G. Ulmer had directed THE BLACK
CAT in 1934, but preferred the relative freedom he found
working on Poverty Row. If nothing else, concocting a film
with a semblance of redeeming artistic value at PRC presented a challenge. Besides, as long as the films came out
within the prescribed budget, and on schedule (normally six
days), no one much cared about the creative decisions. At
PRC, Ulmer was able to create DETOUR (1945), a film that
some consider to be the best "B" film ever made.

In a way, Langdon and "B" films suited each other.
He provided the selling point (his name) and they gave him
a chance to play starring roles. As the star, his routines
became more than incidental flourishes to some larger story;
they were the entire raison d'etre for making (or watching)
the film in the first place.   Langdon was at his best occupy-
ing center stage. His minimalistic reactions were too subtle
to be used well in ensemble playing. He had a talent that
was, essentially, that of an actor performing "in one"--or
with a partner. He rarely made much of an impression in
group scenes or in supporting parts.

Langdon's first in a trio of low-budget features was

MISBEHAVING HUSBANDS (1940) for PRC. The picture was
directed by William Beaudine, another former luminary whose
career had gone from the sublime (D. W. Griffith's Biograph)
to the ridiculous (PRC). He quickly became the quintessential "hack" director, yet his films occasionally bordered on
competence.

The cast was credible: Ralph Byrd, Esther Muir,
Byron Barr (soon to change his name to Gig Young), and
Betty Blythe. Although Harry technically received only third
billing (after Byrd and Muir), he was the key character, had
the most footage, and appeared on the movie poster in three
different poses.

Harry, forever getting into sexual jeopardy, portrayed
department store executive Henry Butler. On his twentieth
wedding anniversary, he is accused of infidelity. His wife
(Blythe), normally a warm and likeable woman, becomes convinced (by some rather flimsy evidence) that her husband is
having an affair. The other woman turned out to be a store
mannequin, hence the alternate title DUMMY TROUBLE (sometimes used on television prints) and the ad line: "Her Rival
Melted in Hubby's Arms!" One of the picture's bigger laughs
undoubtedly occurred when Henry likens the dummy to Hedy
Lamarr, but his associate thinks it resembles Vivien Leigh.
"Vivien WHO?" Harry asks. "Never heard of her!" GONE
WITH THE WIND had been released the year before.

Henry Butler provides the best example of late Langdon in top form, playing a confused, forgetful executive. The
film climaxes as Butler returns home sloshed with the dummy
slung over his shoulder. Naturally, they must climb stairs
together, or try.

Of MISBEHAVING HUSBANDS, Variety wrote:

> About the only redeeming features of this absurd
> comedy drama on the divorce racket are Harry
> Langdon's sprightly comedy characterization and
> Betty Blythe's re-entry to the Hollywood scene as
> a promising actress. The story is mostly wretch-
> edly acted, feebly presented and haphazardly di-
> rected. [1]

The film is better than that, but not much. Variety was quite
correct to point out the excellence of both Langdon and Blythe.
One can truly care about their relationship; although the lesser

elements are qualitatively erratic, the crux of the story remains secure.

DOUBLE TROUBLE is notable for only one thing:
Langdon was re-united with writer/director Charley Rogers.
Rogers had directed Harry during his difficult days with
Roach. Having fallen on lean times himself, Rogers agreed
to co-star as Harry's screen partner. As a gag man for
Laurel and Hardy, Rogers had been in his element. As an
actor, his brittle British persona was workman-like, but
hardly inspiring. Monogram publicity hailed the formation
of "a new comedy team which bids fair to spring into instant
popularity." The studio publicists were, as usual, overly
optimistic. Yet, the two managed to work together fairly
well.

They played British refugees Alfred and Albert Prat-
tle (Langdon, Rogers), who gain passage to America from
the wealthy Whitmores who are under the impression that
they are children. Alf and Bert go to work in Whitmore's
canned bean manufacturing plant, and soon lose a $100,000
diamond in a can of beans. Alf and Bert dress as waitresses
to recover the missing diamond. Langdon and Rogers made
extremely grotesque females.

THE HOUSE OF ERRORS stands as the last feature
that can truly be called a Langdon film. Although his career
wasn't over, this was the last time his name appeared alone
above the title. Langdon contributed the original story (although he did not write the actual screenplay).

THE HOUSE OF ERRORS lacks the ingratiating cast
that elevated MISBEHAVING HUSBANDS above the usual PRC
standards. Most of the actors are wooden and amateurish.
The love story is hopelessly trite. The wisecracking reporter (Ray Walker) amounts to a cardboard stereotype of
the most irritating variety. He sounds like Agent Maxwell
Smart, and his dialogue makes as little sense.

Yet, amid a sad collection of bad actors, Harry Langdon was the consummate professional. His ability remained
undiminished. Sound had diluted it. Poor writing had bat-
tered it. Age had blunted it. Harry still exuded a kind of
magic. He was a trouper in the best sense of the word. He
gave his all, resisting the temptation to walk through a role
in a forgettable film. Through sheer talent, he singlehandedly
transformed a cynically-produced programmer into something

of value. He always knew exactly what he was doing, and it showed.

The war-time plot centers around inventor Hiram Randall's design for an advanced machine gun that will be a major boon to the Allies. Thieves get wind of the invention and decide to steal the prototype that Randall keeps in his home laboratory. Harry and Charley are messenger boys who dream of becoming reporters, and pose as servants in the Randall home to get the scoop on the invention.

Harry's introduction amounts to a pantomime sequence, as he tries to quiet the blaring horn mechanism of his car. All the familiar hesitations and gestures are there, including the necessary tension: Charley is trying to get some sleep.

First, Harry peers into the engine, putting one hand flat above his brow as if he is looking into the sun over a great distance; actually, the engine is about twelve inches away. Then he removes the offensive horn mechanism and shushes it. Amazingly, the horn stops. For about three seconds. He helplessly tries putting it under his work apron, and finally stashes it in a garbage can. In the end, Charley is awakened not by the ear-splitting horn but by the pounding of Harry's hammer as he awkwardly smashes the thing. The routine is beautifully realized, especially since it could never have been accomplished in one of his classic silent films. Sometimes, Harry could find a way to use sound to a distinct advantage.

Harry's reaction to a beautiful woman remained as child-like as ever. When he meets Florence, Randall's beautiful daughter, he swoons; as he sinks to the floor, a "love bird" theme (with tweeting birds) plays on the soundtrack. Harry didn't use the opportunity to replay his famous scene with Joan Crawford in TRAMP, TRAMP, TRAMP. He settled, instead, for a dreamy, drugged expression as Florence left the room.

Another pantomime bit (a play on wartime shortages) shows Harry slinking up to a hidden library safe, and surreptitiously dialing the combination. Opening the safe he removes ... sugar cubes. He drops them into his coffee, tastes, and slyly exits.

[Opposite:] HOUSE OF ERRORS (PRC, 1942, with Ray Walker (right), Langdon, and Charley Rogers (left).

HOUSE OF ERRORS (PRC, 1942), with Charley Rogers.
(Michael Copner Collection)

The major set piece of THE HOUSE OF ERRORS takes
place that same evening, as Harry and Charley are guarding
the gun, all alone in the house. A storm comes up, replete
with lightning and thunder. The fuses blow, and the bumbling
duo have to make do with candle light. As Charley attends
to his knitting, Harry sits nearby growing more and more
frightened by the eerie shadows. Outside, two thieves are
attempting to break into the house to steal the gun.

In one unlikely ploy, they use a slingshot to shoot a
fish hook on a string across the room, hoping to snag the
housekeys which are on the table next to Harry. First they
catch his handkerchief, causing it to fly out of his pocket.
Next they pull off his hat. By this time, Harry's eyes are
growing wider, as he tries to tell his pal that something very
strange is happening in this old dark house.

Charley shrugs all this off as hallucinations resulting from indigestion, urging Harry to go to the kitchen and take some soda and water. Harry doesn't like the stuff. "It goes right to your stomach. If it'll blow up a biscuit, what'll it do to your stomach?" Charley maintains that Harry's problems stem from the combination of pickles, cheese and pie they had for supper.

Finally, the hook snags Harry's shoe. He watches with mounting alarm as his legs repeatedly uncross. When he falls to the floor and gets dragged halfway across the room, he decides that maybe he should have some soda after all.

In THE HOUSE OF ERRORS, Langdon is genuinely funny. Some of the gag sequences are nicely developed, giving Harry a chance to display his reliable comic reflexes. When the fuses blow and the house is dark, some amusing "haunted house" music on the score adds excitement to the action. Betty Blythe, as Randall's wife, contributes a sense of style and good humor.

No actor could have made this last film into a work of art. Perhaps the most unfortunate aspect of Langdon's low budget efforts was its detrimental effect on his creative powers. Not his acting ability; that never flagged. But his contributions to these later scripts never amounted to more than re-hashes of earlier material or uninspired farce. With circumstances constantly forcing him to come up with quick ideas, Harry rarely delivered anything fresh or exciting.

The alternate view, of course, is that Langdon had used all his best ideas years ago, and was creatively burned out. Even with the best of budgets, time for re-takes and re-shooting, experimental previews, and all the other aspects of a high quality production, Langdon might not have had anything new to offer. Could Langdon alone have written a first class script? Some would say no, and there is little evidence to support the opposite view. Barring the highly unlikely discovery of unproduced screenplays of exceptional quality, the answer will always be a matter of conjecture.

Despite all the shortcomings of Langdon's sound films, some film enthusiasts prefer them to the silent comedies, probably for the following reasons: 1) Langdon had an excellent comedy voice. When the scripts went downhill, his

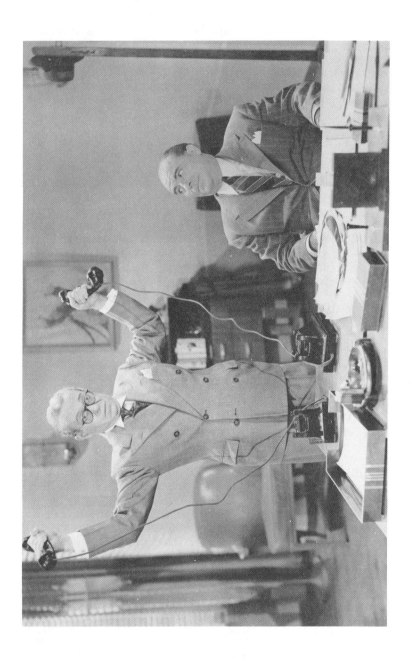

reedy vocal inflections became one of his most reliable laugh-inducers. 2) The sound films generally depended more heav-ily on plot, which makes them easier to follow. The story itself was more important at Columbia than at Sennett. 3) Many could never relate to the Little Elf. Although the Elf embodied certain universal concepts and feelings, the humor was too infantile for some viewers. The dimension of sound rounded out some disquieting, excessive aspects of Langdon's babyish comic persona, although limiting it in the process.

In retrospect, the most interesting aspect of the talkies is that they represent a major portion of his output, for bet-ter or worse. One can regret his lamentable luck, but they are still Harry Langdon films. As the later, perhaps regret-table, efforts of one of the top four silent comedy geniuses, they command attention simply by their very existence.

Many had forgotten his great talent, but his name was remembered. More than that, Langdon was a working actor whose face still appeared on six-foot-high three-sheet posters and on movie screens around the world. He, like other for-mer celebrities, existed on the periphery of the public's con-sciousness. After all, thousands (maybe millions) saw his Columbia shorts, for they were widely distributed and stretched over a ten-year span. Although few would pay to see Lang-don alone, they nevertheless enjoyed him when they saw him.

During the 1940's, Harry was quite satisfied with his lot. He asserted that fame wasn't everything and claimed to be completely serene. He had much of what is considered the good life: a successful marriage, a son, a home, friends, a bank account (after many years of fiscal uncertainty), and enough work to keep him busy. The impression (generally perpetrated by the capsule summaries of his career found in various film histories) that Langdon died a lonely and broken man in poverty and obscurity is a gross misinterpretation of the facts.

When he wasn't commuting to one of the studios, Harry continued his hobby of song-writing, often sitting down at the piano after a hard day in front of the cameras. He sculpted and cartooned. He spent a lot of time remodeling his home

[Opposite:] HOT RHYTHM (Monogram, 1944). (Michael Copner Collection)

to suit his and Mabel's tastes. In Hollywood, many comedians and industry people remembered and respected Harry,
and the Langdons had an active social life. If it wasn't the
life of a superstar, it was a good life anyway. His professional life had undeniable overtones of tragedy; his private
life was nothing short of a triumph. He had survived.

Harry occasionally returned to the stage and appeared
in a few plays during World War II. He auditioned for a
part in the hit Broadway show Hellzapoppin' in 1941, when
the comedy team of Olsen and Johnson left the show. Harry
wanted to replace Johnson, but Happy Felton got the part.
Langdon co-starred with Edith Fellows in Out of the Frying
Pan in 1943.

Harry also signed a contract with RKO studios as a
gag writer. Although Phoebe and Henry Ephron received
credit for the screenplay of BRIDE BY MISTAKE (1944),
Harry contributed several gags but was not given a screen
mention. He also worked on a 1944 unproduced feature that
was to star the Mexican comedian Cantinflas. He probably
wrote anonymously for several other film projects during this
period.

He never gave up trying to resuscitate his movie act-
ing career, but everything after ZENOBIA was anti-climactic.
Langdon was unable to unify and consolidate his audience,
mainly due to the unevenness of most of his talking films.
Only ZENOBIA, HALLELUJAH! I'M A BUM, and SEE AMER-
ICA THIRST rose above "B" film quality. As the decade ad-
vanced, his film opportunities worsened. Just for the work,
Harry sometimes performed in short films for arcades. In
FASHIONS OF 1942, he sings "Beautiful Clothes Make Beauti-
ful Girls"--simply a pretext to parade a series of attractive
models before the casual viewer. Once compared to Chaplin,
Langdon could now be had for a nickel.

He made brief appearances in low-budget musicals.
Westerns and detective stories could be easily adapted to the
cheap production values of Monogram and Republic, but the
musicals (which were always more expensive to make than
comparable dramatic films) proved more difficult to scale
down. The use of popular songs of the day cost too much
money, and the song-writing talent available on Poverty Row
was third-rate at best. These films were usually creaky
vehicles for washed up variety performers, vocalists, and
comics. Langdon's first, SPOTLIGHT REVUE (1943), some-

times called SPOTLIGHT SCANDALS, was directed by William
Beaudine.   Frank Fay, an ex-vaudevillan who had been married to Barbara Stanwyck and appeared on the same bill as
Langdon at the Palace in 1929, teamed up with comedian Billy
Gilbert.   Langdon played a character named Oscar, the butt
of Gilbert and Fay's caustic comments.   Harry was sixth-
billed in what amounted to a cameo role.

In HOT RHYTHM (1944), Harry played recording studio executive Mr. Whiffle, a small part that actually had
several amusing moments.   They all originated in Langdon's
expert comic reflexes.   Whiffle fumbles with multiple telephones, getting tangled in the cords and increasingly more
perplexed.   Again Harry demonstrated that he could spin
straw into gold, if given half a chance.

His last film appearance effectively shows how deeply
he had fallen.   He found himself in another bit part in a Republic musical called SWINGIN' ON A RAINBOW (1945).   As
Chester Willoby, he plays a minor character who helped song-
writer Jane Frazee.   Apart from playing walk-ons[2] and even
smaller parts, there was no place on the screen left for
Harry to go.   But Langdon never had to face that eventuality.
SWINGIN' ON A RAINBOW was his last film.

Death came suddenly and painfully for Harry.   He
hadn't been ill, but he was working hard on the Republic film.
He was taxed physically by a dance routine.   Langdon returned home one evening complaining to Mabel that he had an
unusually bad headache.

She rushed him to a doctor, who confirmed that Harry
was suffering from an unusual form of vascular headache.
Nothing could be done except to administer pain-killers and
hope that it passed.

Harry's condition became critical in a matter of days.
He was then sixty years old, and his body could not take the
strain.   He lapsed into a coma and never regained consciousness.   He had fallen sick on December 8, 1944.   Fourteen days
later, Harry Langdon died of a cerebral hemorrhage.

NOTES

1.   Variety, January 5, 1941.
2.   Gertrude Astor contributed a walk-on to SWINGIN' ON A
     RAINBOW.

Chapter Eighteen: POST MORTEMS

Not only were the 1940's the worst years of Harry Langdon's career, they were bad years for film comedy in general. Eighty percent of all great American screen comedy was produced in the 1920-1940 period, which can be called the Golden Age of Comedy. One can convincingly argue that (with a few exceptions) film comedy has never recovered.

The great silent fantasists were all having troubles by 1940. Harold Lloyd had plunged gamely into the sound era, but by THE MILKY WAY (1936) the real excitement surrounding his films had dissipated. Buster Keaton had stumbled early at M-G-M and worked sporadically in the forties in Columbia shorts and bit parts, only a small notch above Langdon. Chaplin's THE GREAT DICTATOR (1940) was a success, but very soon his turbulent private life (and so-called Communist philosophy) caused the public to turn against him. He never played anything remotely like the Little Tramp again.

Even the early talking comedians were faltering by the advent of World War II. W. C. Fields, perhaps the most important comedian of the 1930's, was ill and played out. The Marx Brothers had started auspiciously, but with their move from Paramount to M-G-M, their films became mere re-makes of earlier hits. Mae West was hampered by the strict production code, and her widespread popularity decreased as her films became tame and predictable. Laurel and Hardy's unfortunate fate at Fox and M-G-M has already been mentioned in Chapter 16.

206

The giants had all fallen. Who came forward to replace them? The two primary comic phenomena of this period were Abbott and Costello and Bob Hope. Though both
had their high points (with Hope occasionally verging on true
genius), their principal métier was verbal humor. In terms
of visual comedy, they often left much to be desired, particularly when compared to the four great silent clowns.

That is just what James Agee (film critic, screen
writer and poet) said in his landmark essay, "Comedy's
Greatest Era." Agee had noticed the decline in screen comedy. His analysis inevitably led him back to those comics
of the silent screen whom he considered most important:
Chaplin, Keaton, Lloyd ... and Langdon. This 1949 essay
became the milestone that marked the beginning of renewed
interest and appreciation for silent comedy in America.
Agee began,

> Even those who have never seen anything better
> must occasionally have the feeling ... that they
> are having to make a little cause for laughter go
> an awfully long way. And anyone who has watched
> screen comedy over the past ten or fifteen years
> is bound to realize that it has quietly but steadily
> deteriorated.

Citing Chaplin and Keaton came as no surprise, but
it is to Agee's credit that he was perceptive enough to include Langdon in his pantheon. Agee's status as the most
influential film critic of the 1940's has caused his respectful
colleagues to take his cue and include Harry among the greats.
Thus, when Professor of Cinema Donald W. McCaffrey wrote
his very thorough and insightful book on silent comedy, he
titled it Four Great Comedians. "Langdon's virtues are
strong enough for a king's robe," McCaffrey wrote. "He
will remain in the king's row with Chaplin, Lloyd and Keaton,
as long as his films are preserved for posterity."

"Comedy's Greatest Era" did more than secure Harry's
place in film history. Agee's essay helped spur interest in
a revival of an art form that many had rejected earlier as
old-fashioned and passé.

On April 8, 1950, Chaplin re-released CITY LIGHTS
(1931). Its reception was truly spectacular, a triumph for
a comedian some said the public had totally spurned. But

Charlie's unpopular political views cast no shadow on the resounding success and praise from the critics. A whole new
generation saw this Chaplin classic and responded as though
it were brand new. If anyone doubted, it was then clear that
silent film would continue to entertain audiences, and that the
tradition was worth preserving.

As the 1950's progressed, silent comedy revivals became a common occurrence in the large cities, although there
was still doubt about how many of the actual films had survived. Lloyd had always had the foresight and financial means
to preserve his films, and personally produced several re-
releases and compilation films into the 1960's. But for a
long time, Keaton believed that many of his greatest films
no longer existed in any form. That Keaton's great work
was found, restored and revived (frequently) is one of the
most significant film events of the 1950's. Like Chaplin and
Lloyd, Keaton won a new audience that (at least among cineastes) nearly rivals the Little Tramp.

Harry Langdon has not been so lucky. While the
others were being re-discovered and re-evaluated, Harry
seemed to get lost in the shuffle. Although nearly all of
Langdon's films were available (with the exception of HEART
TROUBLE), they simply weren't as often or widely revived
as the others. None of them ever received a major re-
release like CITY LIGHTS and THE GENERAL. The reasons
are several.

First, Harry had never made the initial impact of the
other three. Chaplin was on top for a full fifteen to twenty
years; Keaton had his golden decade. Lloyd, too, enjoyed
considerable longevity. And with that kind of longevity comes
the affection and loyalty of fans who had grown up with their
favorites. No one could have grown up with Harry, without
putting in a lot of effort to follow his sound films. Three
years at the top is hardly long enough to build a solid following.

If Harry was not accorded the same fond affection as
Charlie among the older audience, he was an extremely puz-
zling presence to any new viewers who might have caught a
Langdon revival. As has already been discussed, a great
deal of Harry's humor involved subtle parody of the Sennett
style, which was not easily understood by young viewers who
were unfamiliar with the silent comedy tradition.

Finally, and perhaps most significantly, Harry's un-
timely death prevented him from presiding over events. All
the others were healthy and able to actively promote their
resurgences, which they all did with great relish. Only
Harold Lloyd had retired from the screen. Chaplin wrote,
directed, and starred in LIMELIGHT (1952) to much critical
approval (there were a few dissenters) and Keaton made frequent appearances on early television. Harry had only his
wife, Mabel, to represent him. Although she undertook the
task with enthusiasm, collecting films and information and
speaking at revivals, the comedian's wife is not as good a
promoter as the comedian himself.

Aside from sporadic art house revivals, however,
Langdon popped up occasionally in wide-release media. These
appearances were often in the form of brief clips. Probably
the most visible format came with Robert Youngson's com-
pilations such as THE GOLDEN AGE OF COMEDY (1958) and
THE SOUND OF LAUGHTER (1963). These films, and others
like them, brought silent (and early sound) comedy to the
masses. So did syndicated television series like COMEDY
CAPERS, which sometimes featured Langdon along with Snub
Pollard, Charley Chase, and several others. They removed
the titles and added sound effects and musical scores. Both
SMILE PLEASE and REMEMBER WHEN? were trimmed to
ten minutes and released as WATCH THE BIRDIE and LOST
AND FOUND. His later talkies even turned up alongside
Three Stooges films in local television outlets; this was undoubtedly due to the Columbia connection, where both series
were produced. And every so often, on a Saturday afternoon,
a Langdon feature would surface: BLOCK BUSTERS (1944),
Harry's comedy with the East Side Kids, or MISBEHAVING
HUSBANDS (1940). One Seattle station took to showing THE
HOUSE OF ERRORS a dozen times in a three-week period,
along with other PRC films. The common denominator among
all these varieties of media exposure is that you had to look,
and look hard, to see Harry anywhere at all during the Chaplin and Keaton revival years.

The Gallery of Modern Art in New York held a major
Langdon retrospective in December 1967. But the most important Langdon revival occurred when Kino International
sponsored a series called "The Silent Clowns" which was released in a publicity tie-in with Walter Kerr's book. The
first series contained over thirty long and short silent comedy classics. Thus, thousands were introduced to Harry's

best features: TRAMP, TRAMP, TRAMP, THE STRONG
MAN, and LONG PANTS.

Langdon has fared slightly better in film histories and
books discussing silent comedy. Agee set the tone. Significantly, that Agee based much of his Langdon section on the
recollections of Frank Capra (then a big celebrity and Oscar
winner) guided most of the ensuing point of view on the Capra-
Langdon relationship. Since all of the information was from
Capra's side, his portrait of Harry as a gifted but tragic egotist has been widely accepted and repeated.

By far the majority of the material written about Langdon has tended to be repetitive, superficial and in line with
Agee's initial analysis. Certainly Capra's autobiography is
must reading on Langdon and allows the director to tell his
side of the story. A great deal of respect and affection for
Harry comes through, despite some residual bitterness.

The best book on Langdon is The Silent Clowns. Kerr
was a Langdon fan as a boy, and a keen observer who became captivated with the ambiguity of the Little Elf. Kerr
enjoys Langdon, and that enthusiasm comes through in a way
rarely discernible in other competent writings like Gerald
Mast's chapter in The Comic Mind. Both Kerr and Mast
accept the general lines of Capra's point of view, however.

Fortunately, there is hope that Langdon will soon come
out from under Capra's shadow. Film historian Richard Koszarski wrote: "Care should be taken in accepting Capra's
recent self-serving account of Langdon's fall; on the other
hand, there seems some evidence of deliberate distributor
sabotage on the part of First National."[1]

In a less strident tone, Richard Leary wrote in Film
Comment: "Claims for Capra's authorship [of Langdon's
screen character] distort the facts of Langdon's career, and
needlessly denigrate the comic's own sizable talents."[2]
Leland Poague, in The Cinema of Frank Capra, also gives
Langdon much of the credit for his own success. The connection will remain, but a growing number of historians have
begun asserting this revised view of Harry's achievements.

Critics, cineastes and comedy connoisseurs of contemporary times recognize Langdon, acknowledge his talent and
enjoy his films. If Harry never receives widespread public

acceptance again, the fact remains that the cinema has already bestowed on him a kind of immortality.

NOTES

1. Cinema: A Critical Dictionary, 1980, p. 609.
2. Film Comment, November, 1972, p. 15.

SELECTED BIBLIOGRAPHY

BOOKS

Author's Note: Film history has only recently
evaluated the silent era in a substantive manner. Most of the best resources were published in the 1970's.

Agee, James. Agee on Film. New York: McDowell,
Obolensky, Inc., 1958.

Brownlow, Kevin. The Parade's Gone By ... New York:
Alfred A. Knopf, Inc., 1968.

Capra, Frank. The Name Above The Title. New York:
The Macmillan Company, 1971.

Durgnat, Raymond. The Crazy Mirror. New York: Horizon
Press, 1969.

Everson, William K. American Silent Film. New York:
Oxford University Press, Inc., 1978.

Everson, William K. The Films of Laurel and Hardy. New
York: Citadel Press, 1967.

Fowler, Gene. Father Goose. New York: Covici Friede
Publishers, 1934.

Kerr, Walter. The Silent Clowns. New York: Alfred A.
Knopf, 1975.

Koszarski, Richard. Hollywood Directors 1914-1940. New York: Oxford University Press, Inc., 1976.

Lahue, Kalton C. World of Laughter. University of Oklahoma Press, 1972.

Lax, Eric. On Being Funny. New York: Manor Books, Inc., 1975.

McCabe, John. Mr. Laurel and Mr. Hardy. New York: Doubleday, 1960, 1966.

McCaffrey, Donald W. Four Great Comedians. New York: A. S. Barnes & Co., 1968.

Maltin, Leonard. The Great Movie Comedians. New York: Crown Publishers, Inc., 1978.

Maltin, Leonard. The Great Movie Shorts. New York: Crown Publishers, Inc., 1972.

Mast, Gerald. The Comic Mind: Comedy and the Movies. Indianapolis, Ind.: The Bobbs-Merrill, Inc., 1973.

Parish, James Robert (and William T. Leonard). The Funsters. New Rochelle, N.Y.: Arlington House Publishers, 1979.

Poague, Leland A. The Cinema of Frank Capra. New York: A. S. Barnes & Co., Inc., 1975.

Rosenberg, Bernard, editor (w/ Harry Silverstein). The Real Tinsel. New York: Macmillan Co., 1970.

Scherle, Victor, and William Turner Levy. The Films of Frank Capra. New York: Citadel Press, 1977.

Schickel, Richard. The Men Who Made the Movies. New York: Atheneum, 1975.

Sennett, Mack (w/ Cameron Shipp). King of Comedy. New York: Pinnacle Books, 1954.

Shales, Tom, et al. The American Film Heritage. Washington, D.C.: Acropolis Books, Ltd., 1972.

Slide, Anthony. The Idols of Silence. New York: A. S. Barnes & Co., Inc., 1976.

Smith, Bill. The Vaudevillians. New York: Macmillan
   Publishing Co., Inc., 1976.

Tuska, Jon, editor. Close-Up: The Hollywood Director.
   Metuchen, N.J.: Scarecrow Press, Inc., 1978.

Walker, Alexander. The Shattered Silents. New York:
   William Morrow & Co., Inc., 1979.

ARTICLES

Albert, Katherine. "What Happened to Harry Langdon?"
   Photoplay, Feb. 1932, pp. 40, 106.

Hall, Leonard. "Hey! Hey! Harry's Coming Back," Photoplay, June 1929, pp. 59, 102.

Langdon, Harry. "The Serious Side of Comedy Making,"
   Theatre XLVI, December 1927, pp. 22, 78. (Subtitled:
   "Funny scenes and situations are more difficult to create
   than straight drama.")

Leary, Richard. "Capra and Langdon," Film Comment,
   Nov. 1972, pp. 15-17.

North, Jean. "It's No Joke to Be Funny," Photoplay, June
   1925, pp. 86.

Schonert, Vernon L. "Harry Langdon - One of the Screen's
   Foremost Comedians Became a Tragic Figure," Films in
   Review, Oct. 1967, Vol. XVIII, No. 7, pp. 470-485.

Truscott, Harold. "Harry Langdon," The Silent Picture,
   Summer 1972, pp. 2-17. Editor: Anthony Slide.

Waller, Tom. "Langdon's Three's a Crowd Ready on
   August 26th," Moving Picture World, August 13, 1927,
   p. 451.

This filmography is, to the author's knowledge, the most complete and accurate to date. I readily acknowledge the possibility that further research could alter certain details. Films are dated by release date. Harry Langdon appeared on screen in all of these films, except where noted.

MACK SENNETT STUDIOS
(Pathe distribution. Two-reelers except where noted.)

1. PICKING PEACHES (1924). Director: Erle C. Kenton. Titles: J. A. Waldron. Photography: George Spear. Special Photography: Ernie Crockett. With Vernon Dent, Irene Lentz, Alberta Vaughan, Ethel Teare, Dot Farley, and Kewpie Morgan.

2. SMILE PLEASE (1924). Director: Roy Del Ruth. Photography: George Spear. Special Photography: Ernie Crockett. With Madeline Hurlock, Jackie Lucas, Tiny Ward, Jack Cooper, and Alberta Vaughan. Working Title: LOOK PLEASANT.

3. SHANGHAIED LOVERS (1924). Director: Roy Del Ruth. Photography: George Spear. Special Photography: Ernie Crockett. Titles: J. A. Waldron. With Tiny Ward, Andy Clyde, Alice Day, and Kalla Pasha.

4. FLICKERING YOUTH (1924). Director: Erle C. Kenton. Titles: J. A. Waldron. Photography: George Spear and Bob Ladd. Special Photography: Ernie Crockett. With Ray Grey, Carlotte Mineau, Louise Carver, and Alice Day.

5. THE CAT'S MEOW (1924). Director: Roy Del Ruth. Titles: J. A. Waldron. Film Editor: William Hornbeck. Photography: William Williams and Lee Davis. Special Photography: Ernie Crockett. With Lucile Thorndike, Alice Day, Kalla Pasha, Madeline Hurlock, and Tiny Ward.

6. HIS NEW MAMA (1924). Director: Roy Del Ruth. Titles: J. A. Waldron. Film Editor: William Hornbeck. Photography: William Williams. With Madeline Hurlock, Alice Day, Andy Clyde, Tiny Ward, and Jack Cooper.

7. THE FIRST HUNDRED YEARS (1924). Director: Harry Sweet. Titles: J. A. Waldron. Photography: George Crocker and William Williams. With Alice Day, Frank Coleman, Louise Carver, and Madeline Hurlock.

8. THE LUCK O' THE FOOLISH (1924). Director: Harry Edwards. With Kalla Pasha, Madeline Hurlock, Marceline Day, Frank Coleman. Working Title: WATCH OUT.

9. THE HANSOM CABMAN (1924). Director: Harry Edwards. Titles: J. A. Waldron. Film Editor: William Hornbeck. Photography: Vernon Walker and Lee Davis. Special Photography: Ernie Crockett. With Marceline Day, Madeline Hurlock, Leo Sulky, Carlotte Mineau, and Andy Clyde.

10. ALL NIGHT LONG (1924). Director: Harry Edwards. Titles: J. A. Waldron. Film Editor: William Hornbeck. Photography: William Williams and Lee Davis. Story: Vernon Smith and Hal Conklin. Special Photography: Ernie Crockett. With Vernon Dent, Natalie Kingston, and Fanny Kelly. Working Title: OVER HERE.

11. FEET OF MUD (1924). Director: Harry Edwards. Titles: J. A. Waldron. Film Editor: William

Hornbeck. Photography: William Williams and
Lee Davis. Special Photography: Ernie Crockett.
With Florence D. Lee, Natalie Kingston, Yorke
Sherwood, Vernon Dent, and Malcolm Waite.

12. THE SEA SQUAWK (1925). Director: Harry Edwards.
Titles: J. A. Waldron. Film Editor: William
Hornbeck. Photography: George Walker and George
Unholz. Special Photography: Ernie Crockett. With
Bud Ross, Leo Sulky, Eugenia Gilbert, Christian
Frank, and Carlotte Mineau. Working Title: A
SCOTCH BLUE-BELLE.

13. BOOBS IN THE WOOD (1925). Director: Harry Ed-
wards. Titles: J. A. Waldron. Film Editor:
William Hornbeck. Story: Arthur Ripley. Photog-
raphy: William Williams and Lee Davis. Special
Photography: Ernie Crockett. With Marie Astaire,
Vernon Dent, and Leo Willis.

14. HIS MARRIAGE WOW (1925). Director: Harry Ed-
wards. Titles: Felix Adler and A. H. Giebler.
Film Editor: William Hornbeck. Story: Arthur
Ripley. Photography: William Williams and Lee
Davis. Special Photography: Ernie Crockett. With
Natalie Kingston, Vernon Dent, and William McCall.

15. PLAIN CLOTHES (1925). Director: Harry Edwards.
Titles: Felix Adler and A. H. Giebler. Story:
Arthur Ripley and Frank Capra. Film Editor:
William Hornbeck. Photography: William Williams
and Earl Stafford. Special Photography: Ernie
Crockett. With William McCall, Clair Cushman,
Vernon Dent, and Jean Hathaway.

16. REMEMBER WHEN? (1925). Director: Harry Edwards.
Story: Arthur Ripley and Clyde Bruckman. Titles:
Felix Adler and A. H. Giebler. Film Editor:
William Hornbeck. Photography: William Williams
and Lee Davis. Special Photography: Ernie Crock-
ett. With Natalie Kingston and Vernon Dent.

17. HORACE GREELEY, JR. (1925). (Although listed in
the Film Daily Yearbook for 1926, and therefore included here, no other information is available on
this film. Alfred Goulding has been given directing
credit, but it is unverified. Another film, THE

THE SEA SQUAWK (Sennett/Pathe, 1925).   (The Museum of
Modern Art, New York City)

WHITE WING'S BRIDE, has appeared in other filmog-
raphies, attributed to Goulding, but is omitted here
for lack of substantiation.)

18. LUCKY STARS (1925). Director: Harry Edwards.
    Story: Arthur Ripley and Frank Capra. Titles:
    A. H. Giebler. Film Editor: William Hornbeck.
    Photography: George Crocker. Special Photography:
    Ernie Crockett. With Natalie Kingston and Vernon
    Dent. Working Title: THE MEDICINE MAN.

19. THERE HE GOES (1925). Director: Harry Edwards.
    With Peggy Montgomery and Frank Whitson. (Very
    little information is available on this film. A print
    was not available, and it was omitted from the Sen-
    nett Collection. Vernon Schonert in Films in Review
    lists it as a three-reeler.)

20. SATURDAY AFTERNOON (1926). Director: Harry Ed-
    wards. Story: Arthur Ripley and Frank Capra.
    Titles: A. H. Giebler. Film Editor: William
    Hornbeck. Photography: William Williams. Spe-
    cial Photography: Ernie Crockett. With Ruth Hiatt,
    Peggy Montgomery, Alice Ward, and Vernon Dent.
    Three reels.

21. SOLDIER MAN (1926). Director: Harry Edwards.
    Story: Arthur Ripley and Frank Capra. Titles:
    A. H. Giebler. Film Editor: William Hornbeck.
    Photography: William Williams. Special Photog-
    raphy: Ernie Crockett. With Natalie Kingston,
    Frank Whitson, and Vernon Dent. Three reels.
    Working Title: SOLDIER BOY.

22. FIDDLESTICKS (1926). Director: Harry Edwards.
    Story: Arthur Ripley and Frank Capra. Titles:
    Tay Garnett. Film Editor: William Hornbeck.
    Photography: William Williams. Special Photog-
    raphy: Ernie Crockett. With Vernon Dent.

THE HARRY LANGDON CORPORATION
STARRING FEATURES
(released by First National Pictures)

1. TRAMP, TRAMP, TRAMP (1926). Director: Harry
   Edwards. Story: Arthur Ripley and Frank Capra.

Adaptation: Tim Whelan, Hal Conklin, J. Frank Holliday, Gerald Duffy and Murray Roth. Photography:
Elgin Lessley and George Spear. With Joan Crawford,
Alec B. Francis, Brooks Benedict, Tom Murray, Edwards Davis, and Carlton Griffith. Six reels.

2. THE STRONG MAN (1926). Director: Frank Capra.
Story: Arthur Ripley. Adaptation: Tim Whelan,
Tay Garnett, James Langdon, and Hal Conklin. Pho-
tography: Elgin Lessley. With Priscilla Bonner,
Gertrude Astor, Brooks Benedict, Arthur Thalasso,
Robert McKim, William V. Mong. Seven reels.
Working Title: THE YES MAN.

3. LONG PANTS (1927). Director: Frank Capra. Story:
Arthur Ripley. Adaptation: Robert Eddy. Photog-
raphy: Elgin Lessley. With Priscilla Bonner, Alma
Bennett, Gladys Brockwell, Alan Roscoe, and Frankie
Darrow. Six reels.

4. THREE'S A CROWD (1927). Director: Harry Langdon.
Story: Arthur Ripley. Adaptation: James Langdon
and Robert Eddy. Photography: Elgin Lessley. With
Gladys McConnell, Helen Hayward, Cornelius Keefe,
Henry Barrows, Frances Raymond, Agnes Steele, and
Brooks Benedict. Six reels. Pre-Release Publicity
Title: PATCHES.

5. THE CHASER (1928). Director: Harry Langdon. Story:
Arthur Ripley. Adaptation: Clarence Hennecke,
Robert Eddy, and Harry McCoy. Titles: A. H.
Giebler. Photography: Elgin Lessley and Frank
Evans. Film Editor: Alfred DeGaetano. With Gladys
McConnell, Helen Hayward, William (Bud) Jamison,
and Charles Thurston. Six reels.

6. HEART TROUBLE (1928). Director: Harry Langdon.
Story: Arthur Ripley. Adaptation: Earle Rodney
and Clarence Hennecke. Titles: Gordon Bradford.
With Doris Dawson, Lionel Belmore, Madge Hunt,
Bud Jamison, Mark Hamilton, and Nelson McDowell.
Six reels. (No copy is known to exist.)

Langdon also appeared in the following silent feature
films:

7. ELLA CINDERS (1926). A First National Production.

Director: Alfred E. Greene. Story: William Connselman. With Colleen Moore, Lloyd Hughes, Vera Lewis, Doris Baker, Emily Gerdes, and Mike Donlin. Langdon made a brief guest appearance.

8. HIS FIRST FLAME (1927). A Mack Sennett Production. Director: Harry Edwards. Story: Arthur Ripley and Frank Capra. Titles: A. H. Giebler. Film editor: William Hornbeck. With Natalie Kingston, Ruth Hiatt, Vernon Dent, Bud Jamison, Dot Farley, and Christian Frank. Five reels.

All preceding films were silent, presented in theaters with live musical accompaniment. The following films have synchronized sound tracks with dialogue.

HAL ROACH STUDIOS
(two reelers, distributed by MGM)
(produced by Hal Roach)

1. HOTTER THAN HOT (1929). Director: Lewis R. Foster. Story: H. M. Walker. With Thelma Todd, Edgar Kennedy, Frank Austin, and Edith Kramer.

2. SKY BOY (1929). Director: Charles Rogers. Story: Leo McCarey. With Eddie Dunn and Thelma Todd.

3. SKIRT SHY (1930). Director: Charles Rogers. Story: H. M. Walker. With May Wallace, Tom Ricketts, Nancy Dover, and Charlie Hall.

4. THE HEAD GUY (1930). Director: Fred L. Guiol. Story: H. M. Walker. With Thelma Todd, Nancy Dover, Eddie Dunn, and Edgar Kennedy.

5. THE FIGHTING PARSON (1930). Director: Fred Guiol and Charles Rogers. Story: H. M. Walker. With Nancy Dover, Thelma Todd, Eddie Dunn, Leo Willis, and Charlie Hall.

6. THE BIG KICK (1930). Director: Warren Doane. Story: H. M. Walker. With Nancy Dover, Edgar Kennedy, Bob Kortsman, and Sam Lufkin.

7. THE SHRIMP (1930). Director: Charles Rogers. Story:
    H. M. Walker. Photography: Art Lloyd. Film Edi-
    tor: Richard Currier. With Thelma Todd, Nancy
    Drexel, James Mason, and Max Davidson.

8. THE KING (1930). Director: James W. Horne and
    Charles Rogers. Story: H. M. Walker. Film
    Editor: Richard Currier. With Dorothy Granger
    and Thelma Todd.

            EDUCATIONAL FILMS CORPORATION
          (two reelers, distributed by Fox studios)

    The following films were all produced by Arvid
    E. Gillstrom under the "Mermaid Comedies"
    banner.

1. THE BIG FLASH (1932). Director: Arvid E. Gillstrom.
    Story: Robert Vernon and Frank Griffin. With Ver-
    non Dent, Lita Chevret, Ruth Hiatt, Matthew Betz,
    King Baggot, Jack Grey, and Bobby Dunn.

2. TIRED FEET (1933). Director: Arvid E. Gillstrom.
    Story: Robert Vernon and Frank Griffin. With Ver-
    non Dent, Shirley Blake, Maidena Armstrong, Eddie
    Baker, William Irving, and Les Goodwin.

3. THE HITCHHIKER (1933). Director: Arvid E. Gill-
    strom. Story: Robert Vernon and Dean Ward.
    With Vernon Dent, Ruth Clifford, William Irving,
    and Chris Marie Meeker.

4. KNIGHT DUTY (1933). Director: Arvid E. Gillstrom.
    Story: Dean Ward and William Watson. With Vernon
    Dent, Matthew Betz, Lita Chevret, Nell O'Day, Eddie
    Baker, and Billy Engle.

5. TIED FOR LIFE (1933). Director: Arvid E. Gillstrom.
    Story: Dean Ward and Vernon Dent. With Vernon
    Dent, Nell O'Day, Mabel Forrest, Elaine Whipple,
    and Eddie Baker.

6. HOOKS AND JABS (1933). Director: Arvid E. Gill-
    strom. Story: Dean Ward and Vernon Dent. With
    Vernon Dent, Nell O'Day, William Irving, and Frank
    Moran.

7. THE STAGE HAND (1933). Director: Harry Langdon. Story: Harry Langdon and Edward Davis. With Marel Foster, Eddie Schubert, and Ira Hayward.

8. TRIMMED IN FURS (1933). Director: Charles Lamont. Story: Ernest Pagano and Ewart Adamson. With John Sheehan, Eleanor Hunt, Dorothy Dix, Louise Keaton, Tom Francis, Harold Berquist, Neal Pratt, Faye Pierre.

PARAMOUNT PRODUCTIONS
(two-reel comedies)

The following films were produced by
Arvid E. Gillstrom.

9. MARRIAGE HUMOR (1933). Director: Harry Edwards. Story: Dean Ward and Vernon Dent. With Vernon Dent, Nancy Dover, Ethel Sykes, and Eddie Schubert.

10. ON ICE (1933). Director: Arvid E. Gillstrom. Story: Dean Ward and Vernon Dent. With Vernon Dent, Eleanor Hunt, Ethel Sykes, Kewpie Morgan, Ruth Clifford, Diana Seaby, and William Irving.

11. ROAMING ROMEO (1933). Director: Arvid E. Gillstrom. Story: Dean Ward and Vernon Dent. With Vernon Dent, Nell O'Day, Jack Henderson, and Les Goodwin.

12. CIRCUS HOODOO (1934). Director: Arvid E. Gillstrom. Story: Dean Ward and Vernon Dent. With Vernon Dent, Eleanor Hunt, Matthew Betz, Diana Seaby, James Morton, and Tom Kennedy.

13. PETTING PREFERRED (1934). Director: Arvid E. Gillstrom. Story: Jack Townley. Adaptation: Dean Ward and Vernon Dent. With Vernon Dent, Dorothy Granger, Eddie Baker, and Alice Ardell.

In 1933, Langdon appeared in one of a series of Paramount shorts called HOLLYWOOD ON PARADE (produced by Louis Lewyn). He contributed a golfing skit with Viola Dana.

COLUMBIA PICTURES
(two reel comedies)

The following films were produced by Jules White.

1. COUNSEL ON DE FENCE (1934). Director: Arthur
   Ripley. Story: Harry McCoy. With Renee Whitney,
   Earle Foxe, Jack Norton, Babe Kane, Robert Frazer,
   and Harrison Greene. Working Title: THE BAR-
   RISTER.

2. SHIVERS (1934). Director: Arthur Ripley. Story:
   Arthur Ripley. Screenplay: John Grey. With Flor-
   ence Lake, Dick Elliott, Chester Gan, and Louise
   Vincenot.

3. HIS BRIDAL SWEET (1935). Director: Alfred Goulding.
   Story: John Grey. With Billy Gilbert and Geneva
   Mitchell.

4. THE LEATHER NECKER (1935). Director: Arthur Ripley. Story: Arthur Ripley. Screenplay: John Grey
   and Al Biebler. With Wade Boteler.

5. HIS MARRIAGE MIX-UP (1935). Director: Preston
   Black. Story: Vernon Dent. With Dorothy Granger.
   (Preston Black was a pseudonym for Jack White,
   brother of producer Jules White.)

6. I DON'T REMEMBER (1935). Director: Preston Black.
   Story: Preston Black. With Vernon Dent, Geneva
   Mitchell, Mary Carr, Robert Burns, and Gertrude
   Astor.

7. A DOGGONE MIXUP (1938). Director: Charles Lamont.
   Story: Elwood Ullman, Al Biebler and Charlie Nelson.
   With Ann Doran, Vernon Dent, Bud Jamison, Eddie
   Fetherstone, Bess Flowers, Sarah Edwards, and James
   C. Morton. Working Title: NO SALES RESISTANCE.

8. SUE MY LAWYER (1938). Director: Jules White. Story:
   Harry Langdon. Screenplay: Ewart Adamson. Film
   Editor: Charles Nelson. Photography: George Meehan.
   With Ann Doran, Monty Collins, Bud Jamison, Vernon
   Dent, Cy Schindell, and Don Brodie.

9. COLD TURKEY (1940). Director: Del Lord. Story:

Elwood Ullmann and Harry Edwards. With Ann
Doran, Monty Collins, Vernon Dent, Bud Jamison,
and Eddie Laughton.

10. WHAT MAKES LIZZY DIZZY? (1942). Director: Jules
White. With Elsie Ames, Dorothy Appleby, Monty
Collins, Bud Jamison, Lorin Baker, and Kathryn
Sabichi.

11. TIREMAN, SPARE MY TIRES (1942). Director: Jules
White. Story: Felix Adler. Screenplay: Clyde
Bruckman. Photography: Benjamin Kline. Film
Editor: Jerome Thoms. A comedy version of IT
HAPPENED ONE NIGHT. Working Title: HONEY-
MOON BLACKOUT.

12. CARRY HARRY (1942). Director: Harry Edwards.
With Elsie Ames, Barbara Pepper, Marjorie Deanne,
Dave O'Brien, and Stanley Blystone.

13. PIANO MOONER (1942). Director: Harry Edwards.
Story: Harry Langdon. With Fifi D'Orsay, Gwen
Kenyon, Betty Blythe, Stanley Blystone, and Chester
Conklin.

14. A BLITZ ON THE FRITZ (1943). Director: Jules
White. Story: Clyde Bruckman. With Louise
Currie, Vernon Dent, Douglas Leavitt, and Bud
Fine. Working Title: SWAT THAT SPY.

15. BLONDE AND GROOM (1943). Director: Harry Edwards. Story: Harry Langdon.

16. HERE COMES MR. ZERK (1943). Director: Jules
White. Story: Jack White. Working Title: SUE
YOU LATER.

17. TO HEIR IS HUMAN (1944). Director: Harry Edwards.
Story: Elwood Ullman and Monty Collins. With Una
Merkel, Vernon Dent, Christine McIntyre, Eddie
Bribbon, Lew Kelly, and John Tyrrell.

18. DEFECTIVE DETECTIVES (1944). Director: Harry
Edwards. Story: Harry Edwards. With El Brendel,
Christine McIntyre, Vernon Dent, Eddie Laughton,
John Tyrrell, Snub Pollard, and Dick Botiller.

19. MOPEY DOPE (1944). Director: Del Lord. Story and
    screenplay: Del Lord and Elwood Ullman. With El
    Brendel, Christine McIntyre, and Arthur Q. Bryan.

20. SNOOPER SERVICE (1945). Director: Harry Edwards.
    Story: Harry Edwards. With El Brendel, Vernon
    Dent, Rebel Randall, Dick Curtis, Fred Kelsey, and
    Buddy Yarus.

21. PISTOL PACKIN' NITWITS (1945). Director: Harry
    Edwards. Story: Edward Bernds and Harry Lang-
    don. Screenplay: Harry Edwards. With El Bren-
    del, Christine McIntyre, Dick Curtis, Tex Cooper,
    Vernon Dent and Heinie Conklin.

MISCELLANEOUS SHORT FILMS

1. GOODNESS! A GHOST (1940). An RKO Radio Produc-
   tion. Director: Harry D'Arcy. Producer: Lou
   Brock. Story: George Jeske and Arthur V. Jones.
   Screenplay: Harry Langdon. Photography: Harry
   Wild. Film Editor: John Lockert. With Harold
   Daniels, Diane Hunter, Robert Stanton, Herbert Clif-
   ton, Tiny Sanford, Jim Morton, and Carl Fremanson.

2. SITTING PRETTY (1940). Produced by Jam Handy
   Picture Service.

3. FASHIONS OF 1942. Harry sang "Beautiful Clothes
   Make Beautiful Girls" for this short (ten minutes)
   which was shown in penny arcades. There are
   probably others like it.

FEATURE FILM APPEARANCES
(1930-1945)

1. A SOLDIER'S PLAYTHING (1930). Warner Brothers.
   Director: Michael Curtiz. Original story: Vina
   Delmar. Screen adaptation: Perry Vekroff. Dia-
   logue: Arthur Caesar. With Lotti Loder, Ben Lyon,
   Jean Hersholt, Noah Beery, Fred Kohler, and Marie
   Astaire. Six reels. Working Title: COME EASY.

2. SEE AMERICA THIRST (1930). Universal. Director:
   William James Craft. Story and dialogue: Edward

I. Luddy and Vin Moore. Adaptation: C. Jerome Horwin. With Slim Summerville, Bessie Love, Mitchell Lewis, Matthew Betz, Stanley Fields, Lloyd Whitlock, Dick Alexander, Tom Kennedy, Lew Hearn, Leroy Mason. Eight reels.

3. HALLELUJAH! I'M A BUM (1933). United Artists. Director: Lewis Milestone. Based on an original story by Ben Hecht. Adaptation: S. N. Behrman. With Al Jolson, Frank Morgan, Madge Evans, Chester Conklin, Tyler Brooke, Tammany Young, Edgar Connor, Dorothea Wolbert, and Louise Carver. British Title: HALLELUJAH! I'M A TRAMP. Nine reels.

4. MY WEAKNESS (1933). Fox. Director: David Butler. Story and dialogue: B. G. De Sylva. Continuity: D. Butler. Music and lyrics: B. G. De Sylva, Leo Robin and Richard Whiting. With Lilian Harvey, Lew Ayres, Charles Butterworld, Sid Silvers, Irene Bentley, Henry Travers, Adrian Rosley, Mary Howard, Irene Ware, Barbara Weeks, and Susan Fleming. Nine reels.

5. ATLANTIC ADVENTURE (1935). Columbia. Director: Albert S. Rogell. Story: Diana Bourbon. Screenplay: John T. Neville and Nat Dorfman. Photography: John Stumar. Film Editor: Ted Kent. With Nancy Carroll, Lloyd Nolan, E. E. Clive, Dwight Frye, John Wray, Vivian Oakland, Robert Middlemass, and Arthur Hohl. Seven reels.

6. HE LOVED AN ACTRESS (1938). Biltmore Pictures. Distributed by Grand National in U.S.A. Producer: William Rowland. Director: Melville Brown. Story: John F. Harding. Screenplay: John Meehan, Jr. With Lupe Velez, Ben Lyon, Wallace Ford, Jean Colin, Mary Cole, Cyril Raymond, Ronald Ward, Olive Sloane, Arthur Finn, and Peggy Novak. British Titles: STARDUST, MAD ABOUT MONEY. Released in England in 1937.

7. THERE GOES MY HEART (1938). Hal Roach. Producer: Milton H. Bren. Director: Norman Z. McLeod. Story: Ed Sullivan. Screenplay: Jack Jevne and Eddie Moran. Photography: Norbert Brodine. Film Editor: William Termune. Photographic effects: Roy Seawright. With Fredric March, Virginia Bruce,

Langdon and Jolson in HALLELUJAH! I'M A BUM (United
Artists, 1933). (William Schelly Collection)

Patsy Kelly, Alan Mowbray, Nancy Carroll, Eugene
Pallette, Calude Gillingwater, Etienne Girardot, Irving Bacon, Arthur Lake, and Irving Pichel.

8. ZENOBIA (1939). United Artists/Hal Roach. Producer:
    Edward Sutherland. Director: Gordon Douglas.
    Original Story: Walter DeLeon and Arnold Belgard.
    Screenplay: Corey Ford. Photography: Karl Struss.
    Film Editor: Bert Jordan. With Oliver Hardy, Billie
    Burke, Alice Brady, Stepin Fetchit, James Ellison,
    Jean Parker, June Lang, Hattie McDaniel, Olin How-
    land, J. Farrell MacDonald, and Phillip Hurlic.
    (Langdon received second billing, after Hardy.) Brit-
    ish Title: ELEPHANTS NEVER FORGET. Working
    Title: IT'S SPRING AGAIN.

9. MISBEHAVING HUSBANDS (1940). Producers Releasing
    Corporation. Producer: Jed Buell. Director:

William Beaudine. Story: Cea Sabin. Screenplay:
Vernon Smith and Claire Parrish. With Betty Blythe,
Ralph Byrd, Esther Muir, Cayne Whitman, Florence
Wright, Luana Walters, Charlotte Treadway, Frank
Jacquet, Byron Barr, Frank Havney, Hennie Brown,
and Billy Mitchell.

10. ALL-AMERICAN CO-ED (1941). United Artists/Hal
     Roach. Producer: Leroy Prinz. Director: Leroy
     Prinz. Original Story: Leroy Prinz and Hal Roach,
     Jr. Screenplay: Cortland Fitzsimmons. Adaptation:
     Kenneth Higgins. Photography: Robert Pittack.
     Film Editor: Bert Jordan. Songs: Walter G. Sam-
     uels, Charles Newman and Lloyd R. Norlin. With
     Frances Langford, Johnny Downs, Marjorie Wood-
     worth, Noah Beery, Jr. , Esther Dale, Alan Hale,
     Jr. , Kent Rogers, Allan Lane, Joe Brown, Jr. ,
     Irving Mitchell, Lillian Randolph, and Carlyle Black-
     well, Jr.

11. DOUBLE TROUBLE (1941). Monogram. Producer:
     Dixon R. Harwin. Associate Producer: Barney
     Sarecky. Director: William West. Screenplay:
     Jack Natteford. Film Editor: Carl Pierson. Pho-
     tography: A. Martinelli. With Charles Rogers,
     Catherine Lewis, Dave O'Brien, Frank Jaquet, Mira
     McKinney, Wheeler Oakman, Louise Curry, Benny
     Rubin, and Edward Kane.

12. HOUSE OF ERRORS (1942). Producers Releasing Cor-
     poration. Producer: George R. Batcheller and
     Bernard B. Ray. Director: Bernard B. Ray.
     Story: Harry Langdon. Screenplay: Ewart Adam-
     son and Eddie M. Davis. With Charles Rogers,
     Marian Marsh, Ray Walker, John Holland, Betty
     Blythe, and Vernon Dent.

13. SPOTLIGHT REVUE (1943). Monogram. Producer:
     Sam Katzman and Jack Dietz. Director: William
     Beaudine. Musical Director: Edward Kay. Film
     Editor: Carl Pierson. Photography: Mack Stengler.
     Art Director: Dave Milton. With Billy Gilbert,
     Frank Fay, Bonnie Baker, Billy Lenhradt, Charles
     K. Brown, Iris Adrian, James Bush, Claudia Dell,
     Eddie Parks, Betty Blythe, Henry King, and Herb
     Miller. Also known as SPOTLIGHT SCANDALS.

14. HOT RHYTHM (1944). Monogram. Producer: Lindsley
    Parsons. Director: William Beaudine. Story and
    screenplay: Tim Ryan and Charles Marion. Film
    Editor: Richard Currier. Musical Director: Ed-
    ward Kay. With Robert Lowery, Tim Ryan, Irene
    Ryan, Dona Drake, Sidney Miller, Robert Kent,
    Jerry Cooper, Lloyd Ingraham, Cyril Ring, Joan
    Curtis, and Paul Porcasi.

15. BLOCK BUSTERS (1944). Monogram. Producer: Sam
    Katzman and Jack Dietz. Director: Wallace Fox.
    Assistant Director: Arthur Hammond. Film Editor:
    Carl Pierson. Photography: Marcel Le Picard.
    Original Story: Houston Branch. With Leo Gorcey,
    Huntz Hall, Gabriel Dell, Billy Benedict, Jimmy
    Strand, Bill Chaney, Minerva Urecal, Roberta Smith,
    Noah Beery, Sr. , Fred Pressel, Jack Gilman, Kay
    Marvis, and Charles Murray, Jr.

16. SWINGIN' ON A RAINBOW (1945). Republic. Producer:
    Eddy White. Director: William Beaudine. Story:
    Olive Cooper. Screenplay: Olive Cooper and John
    Grey. Photography: Marcel LePicard. Film Editor:
    Fred Allen. Musical Director: Morton Scott. With
    Jane Frazee, Brad Taylor, Amelita Ward, Minna
    Gombell, Richard Davies, Tim Ryan, Wendell Niles,
    Paul Harvey, and Gertrude Astor.

HARRY LANGDON WRITING CREDITS

Langdon did not appear in any of the following films.

1. BLOCKHEADS (1938). A Stan Laurel Production for Hal
   Roach. Director: John G. Blystone. Screenplay:
   James Parrott, Harry Langdon, Felix Adler, Charles
   Rogers and Arnold Belgard. Photography: Art Lloyd.
   With Laurel and Hardy, Billy Gilbert, Patricia Ellis,
   James Finlayson, Minna Gombell, Harry Woods,
   Harry Stubbs, and William Royle.

2. THE FLYING DEUCES (1939). An RKO-Radio Production.
   Producer: Boris Morros. Director: Edward Suther-
   land. Screenplay: Ralph Spence, Harry Langdon,
   Charles Rogers and Alfred Schiller. Photography:
   Art Lloyd and Elmer Dyer (aerial photography). Film
   Editor: Jack Dennis. With Laurel and Hardy, Jean

Publicity photo for HEART TROUBLE (First National, 1928).
(William Schelly Collection)

Parker, Reginald Gardiner, Charles Middleton, James
Finlayson, Jean Del Val, and Clem Wilenchick.
Sketch of Laurel and Hardy in an opening scene by
Harry Langdon.

3. A CHUMP AT OXFORD (1940).   United Artists/Hal
    Roach.   Director: Alfred Goulding.   Screenplay:
    Charles Rogers, Harry Langdon and Felix Adler.
    Photography: Art Lloyd.   Film Editor: Bert Jordan.
    With Laurel and Hardy, Forrester Harvey, James
    Finlayson, Wilfrid Lucas, Forbes Murray, Frank
    Baker, Eddie Borden, Gerald Rogers, Peter Cushing,
    Victor Kendall, Gerald Fielding, and Charles Hall.

4. SAPS AT SEA (1940).   United Artists/Hal Roach.   Di-
    rector: Gordon Douglas.   Screenplay: Charles Rogers,
    Harry Langdon, Gil Pratt and Felix Adler.   Photog-
    raphy: Art Lloyd.   Film Editor: William Ziegler.
    With Laurel and Hardy, James Finlayson, Dick Cramer,
    Ben Turpin, Harry Bernard, and Eddie Conrad.

5. ROAD SHOW (1940).   United Artists/Hal Roach.   Di-
    rector: Hal Roach.   From a novel by Eric Hatch.
    Screenplay: Arnold Belgard, Harry Langdon and
    Mickell Novak.   Photography: Norbert Brodine.   With
    Adolphe Menjou, Carole Landis, John Hubbard, Charles
    Butterworth, Patsy Kelly, George E. Stone.

6. BRIDE BY MISTAKE (1944).   An RKO Production.   Pro-
    ducer: Bert Granet.   Director: Richard Wallace.
    Story: Norman Krasna.   Screenplay: Phoebe and
    Henry Ephron.   Photography: Nicholas Musurace.
    With Alan Marshall, Laraine Day, Marsha Hunt, Allyn
    Joslyn, Edgar Buchanan, Michael St. Angel, Marc
    Cramer, and Slim Summerville.   (Harry Langdon did
    not receive credit for contributing gags to this pic-
    ture.)